Robert Seton Lawrence
Examiner in Speech and Drama at the
London Academy of Music and Dramatic Art

A Guide to Speaking in Public

Revised edition of *A Guide to Public Speaking*

Pan Books London and Sydney

First published 1957 as *A Guide to Public Speaking* by
The World's Work Ltd
Published 1961 as a Cedar Book
Expanded edition published 1964 by Pan Books Ltd
(5 printings)
Revised edition first published 1979 as *A Guide to Speaking in Public* by
Pan Books Ltd, Cavaye Place, London SW10 9PG
2nd printing 1981
© Robert Seton Lawrence 1957, 1976, 1979
ISBN 0 330 25803 6
(1st Pan edition 0 330 02136 2)
Printed and bound in Great Britain by
Richard Clay (The Chaucer Press) Ltd, Bungay, Suffolk

Contents

Part One
Planning and Building the Speech

Part Two
For the More Experienced Speaker

Part Three
Speech and Voice Production

Foreword

I had often been asked to recommend a book on public speaking, simple enough for a beginner to work from on his own, and sufficiently comprehensive to put him, when he had read it, on a firm basis from which to extend his technique.

To meet this need I wrote this book, using the substance of a year's work in theory and practical tutorials with evening classes on the subject.

This Pan edition has been revised to contain details of and advice about entering for public examinations in public speaking and oral English in general. These are held at frequent intervals at convenient centres throughout the British Isles. I strongly advise the aspiring speaker to attempt an examination, for I believe every student should set himself a target and try to get tangible proof of a standard obtained.

This new edition also contains a section for the more experienced speaker.

Robert Seton Lawrence

'The question is,' said Alice, 'whether words can be made to mean so many different things.'

'The question is,' replied Humpty Dumpty, '*who is to be master*, that's all.'

Lewis Carroll

PART ONE
PLANNING AND BUILDING THE SPEECH

THE MAKING OF A PUBLIC SPEAKER

As the adult evolves from the child so the accomplished speaker is formed over years of language experience. The beginning does much to shape the end. In this sense we are *all* public speakers and we extend the frontiers of communication by a process so gradual that we are hardly aware of it.

Language grows from our first infant attempts to communicate in sound immediate and urgent requirements for food, comfort and affection, extending naturally to fractured expressions of pleasure, amusement and curiosity, interspersed with shrill rejection. As vocabulary is acquired and extended links are formed with the external world and a distinctive personality makes its appearance. In proportion to the language-stimulus he receives at this time the child is able to express his feelings more clearly. Where his experience of adult language has been satisfactorily varied, his own resources grow proportionally and his use of words becomes more sophisticated and effective. Later, education – in its widest sense – adds logical arrangement and some ability to use abstract thought.

The adult of reasonable education will, therefore, have gained several kinds of vocabulary:

(*a*) A 'working' vocabulary, including idiom and the abbreviated speech most people use in casual conversation.

(*b*) A 'stored' vocabulary of words we have heard and understand but seldom use.

(*c*) A technical vocabulary concerned with our work – such as might be used by doctors, scientists, engineers, psychologists or social workers.

As education is extended by reading, conversation and experience, so our store of words – and particularly those in everyday use – is multiplied.

Conversely, we should consciously prune our vocabulary

from time to time so as to eliminate tiresome, vague and 'trendy' expressions such as 'at the end of the day', 'at this moment *in time*', 'in this day and age', 'time is of the essence', 'having said that' (a superfluous remark if ever there was one), and many others we can identify for ourselves.

The value of 'small-talk' is not to be despised. It is a kind of oral plasticine with which we make light and usually transient human links. The 'Morning, Mr Jones; nice day', said in passing is the human equivalent of the dog's wagging tail; such statements of the obvious are expressions of goodwill without commitment to further confidences, though these are not excluded. In his search for material the public speaker will find such unpromising openings may lead to extremely interesting conversations.

It is when language is used on a deeper and emotional level that we must be careful, for emotive language is sometimes the 'feeler' we use to judge the trustworthiness and strength of affection between others and ourselves. A clumsy comment can damage a valuable relationship or even make us seem ridiculous. One thinks of Boswell's unfortunate use of words in conversation with the redoubtable Dr Johnson when he said: 'I do indeed come from Scotland, sir, *but I cannot help it.*'

The poet Coleridge defined prose as 'words in their best order' and poetry as 'the *best* words in the best order'. We may do well to remember such a succinct yet comprehensive definition.

The man who cannot distinguish the stark prose of 'It will soon be dawn' from the exquisite lyricism of 'Night's candles are burnt out, and jocund day stands tiptoe on the misty mountain-tops', has much still to learn about language. The aspiring public-speaker must strive to develop sensitivity to words and an easy command of language *in all its forms* if he is to reach into the hearts of his audience. Knowing many words is not enough. It is in their order, weight, colour, and variety, their delicate nuances and inflections and, above all, in their *phrasing*, that magic lies. A teacher who can inspire

14

others with this appreciation and can draw from his students a natural response – always with regard to the preservation of their individuality – is a jewel to be cherished. A mere 'instructor' creates obedient imitators below the reach of artistry.

HOW TO HELP CHILDREN

From their first attempts at language, it is important to speak *with* children rather than *at* them. To acquire a sense of complete expression, children should hear ideas communicated in complete sentences and be encouraged to reply in the same way, however simple their replies may be. The use of abbreviated language, including the ubiquitous 'baby-talk', negates this aim. They should also be encouraged to offer simple explanations. '*Tell* me how this works', does not exclude a demonstration but adds to its effect. Facility is essential to future growth, and demonstration should be linked with thought. Comprehension is very important indeed. Any adjudicator or examiner in speech and drama will confirm that it is only too common to hear students *of all ages* speak poetry, for example, clearly and musically but with little idea of the poet's intention; this is an obedient and imitative recitation, not an artistic interpretation.

It is good to tell stories to little children and even better to pretend, some time later, to have forgotten or become confused about some details of the story and ask them to tell it to you from memory. The really imaginative child will make up his own stories and will often turn them into a serial concerning the adventures of an imagined character. My own daughter told her young brother – in serial form – the adventures of Goblin Glum, a story which ran for weeks and was gaily added to by all the family in turn. Parallel to these prose adventures, an experience of simple verse introduces children to rhyme and rhythm and lays a useful foundation for more advanced discovery later.

Comprehension is aided by occasional simple questions

15

such as 'What do you think he meant by that? What do you think he will do now? What would you do and why?' These unforced questions help to stimulate the child's imagination and concentrate his thoughts on a particular aspect, but there should be no demand for a reply, nor any hint of disappointment or reproof if the child is unable or unwilling to give one.

Ruth and Helen, sisters, from an educated background, were each asked to read a story 'The Lion At School' by Philippa Pearce from a volume called *Stories For Five-Year-Olds and Other Young Readers* edited by Sara and Stephen Corrin (published by Faber and Faber) and were then asked to re-tell the story as they remembered it, with the following result:

Ruth (Aged 8 years)

MOTHER You have been reading a story, Ruth. What is it called?

RUTH 'The Lion At School'.

MOTHER Can you tell me all about it? In your own words. What is the story about? Can you remember how it began?

RUTH The girl didn't like going to school and she had to hurry but she didn't.

MOTHER You mean she was late ... every day?

RUTH No, just that time.

MOTHER I see. What happened?

RUTH She was turning the corner and she found a lion and the lion said, 'I am going to eat you,' and the girl started crying. The lion said, 'I am not finished,' and he said, 'I am going to eat you unless you take me to school with you.' The girl stopped crying and the lion said, 'Shall we go then?' Then she said, 'Yes,' so they went to school. (Long pause)

MOTHER How did they get to school?

RUTH The little girl said, 'You must promise me two things. The first thing is you mustn't eat anybody up; it is not allowed.' And the lion said, 'What is the

16

second thing?' 'Well,' she said, 'can I ride on your back to school?' (Pause)

MOTHER And did she?

RUTH Yes. (Pause)

MOTHER So that is how they got to school. And what happened next?

RUTH The lady read out the register and the lady ... the teacher ... she said ... she came to the girl's name. (Pause)

MOTHER What was the girl's name?

RUTH I can't remember.

MOTHER It doesn't matter. She was reading the register?

RUTH Yes. When she stopped she found the lion and the little girl and she said, 'You're not allowed to bring pets to school,' and she said very quickly, 'He's not a pet, this is my friend.' Then she said, 'What's his name?' 'Noil, just Noil, that's his name – Noil.'

MOTHER That's a funny name. Why did she think of Noil?

RUTH Because she turned the lion backwards to Noil ... Noil, and then she called out the girl's name again and she came to Noil and she wrote Noil down and said 'Noil' and Noil said, 'Yes.' Then the lady, the teacher, said out loud ... she said a story to the children out loud and then they drawed and wrote until dinner time. Then Noil was hungry so he wanted to draw a picture of his dinner. (Pause)

MOTHER Did he draw a picture of dinner?

RUTH Yes. He said, 'What is for dinner? I hope it's meat.' 'No,' said the little girl, 'it's fish-fingers 'cos today is Friday.' So the little girl showed the lion how to draw, how to hold the yellow crayon in his paws and then how to draw fish-fingers, so he wrote fish fingers then the dinner bell went. Everybody went out to play and then they stood in a corner. (Pause)

MOTHER Who stood in a corner?

RUTH The lion and the girl.

MOTHER Why did they stand in a corner?

RUTH   Then the lion said, 'Let's play like the others.' The little girl said, 'No, I don't like playing 'cos some of the boys knock me over on purpose ...' (Pause)

MOTHER   What did the lion say then?

RUTH   'They won't knock you over while *I'm* here.' Then the little girl said, 'There's one boy ... the biggest boy ... who knocks me over on purpose.' The lion said, 'Point him out to me,' so the little girl pointed him out to the lion. The lion said, 'So *that's* the boy; what's his name?' And the little girl said, 'Jack Tall, that's his name, Jack Tall.' And then Jack Tall was coming towards the little girl and the lion in a circle. He was running closer and closer. Then the lion roared and Jack Tall saw his teeth as skewers and knives. The lion roared and roared and all the teachers came out to see what was happening. Then Jack Tall ran towards the playground and then round to the school gates. He ran and ran and ran till he got home to his mother. Then the little girl said, 'I don't think much of *him*.' And then she said, 'It's afternoon school now,' and the lion said, 'I'm not staying for afternoon school.' He went off and the girl said, 'See you on Monday,' but the lion didn't answer, so on Monday the girl was looking forward for Monday so she went to school on Monday in very good time. She went into the classroom and found the lion wasn't there and the teacher read out the register and when she came to the lion's name Noil didn't answer because he wasn't there. Then it came to playtime and Jack Tall came to the little girl and said, 'Where's your friend the lion that roared so loudly?' And the little girl said, 'He's not here, so just watch out, Jack Tall,' and that's the end.

MOTHER   Why should Jack Tall watch out if the lion wasn't there?

RUTH   Because he might knock the girl over.

MOTHER Who – Jack Tall?
RUTH Yes.

Helen (11 years, 1 month)
HELEN It is about a lion and a girl. The girl was always late
getting to school and she was late this day and she
came round the corner on her way to school and saw
a lion and the lion wanted her to take her to school.
MOTHER The lion wanted to take *her* to school?
HELEN The lion wanted the girl to take *him* to school. She
said she would take him to school so long as he
didn't eat anybody up. It wasn't allowed. When they
got to school – late, of course, although they ran –
the lion ran with the girl on his back – the teacher
was calling the register and asked the girl what the
lion's name was and why she brought her pet to
school. The girl said it wasn't a pet, only a friend
that she brought to school and that the lion's name
was Noil as she couldn't tell her really that it was a
lion, so she put lion backwards – Noil. And they did
some work. Then in the playground the girl stood
beside the lion in a corner. The lion asked her why
she wasn't playing with the others. The little girl
said because the other boys ... or some boys would
push her around and push her over accidentally because they were so rough. The lion said, 'Well, they
wouldn't push *me* over.' Then the bell rang and
they went back into school and they had dinner and
drew and that. Then they went into the playground
again and they never played with anybody. Then the
biggest boy, Jack Tall, came up to the little girl and
started running round her, closer and closer, and the
little girl said, 'Stop it! stop it!' And the lion said,
'Don't keep running round my friend or you will
knock her over.' And the biggest boy said, 'Shan't.'
The lion roared and he opened his mouth so wide
that the biggest boy, Jack Tall, saw his sharp teeth

19

and they stood still and stared at him and then he ran away and they went back into school. The lion did not go because he wouldn't stay at school for afternoon school and the little girl said, 'I'll see you on Monday, then,' and the lion just carried on walking. But when she got to school on Monday the little girl never saw the lion and Jack Tall came up to the little girl and said, 'Where's your friend today?' The little girl said, 'He didn't come today.' The boy said, 'Might he come again?' and the little girl said, 'He might, he might just well come, Jack Tall, so watch out,' and that is the end.

The most immediately apparent difference between Ruth's story and Helen's is in the comparative fluency of their separate accounts, each recorded without the presence of the other. The older child appears to have grasped the outline of the story quickly and easily and relates it with very little hesitation and, at times, in a rather detached and off-hand manner. However, she does show more animation in her last paragraph and is clearly aware that this is a climax, that the little girl has gained the upper hand over the bully, Jack Tall, because her friend, the lion, might turn up at any time to defend her.

Ruth's account is much more hesitant and full of long pauses, during which she appears to be trying to gather together the threads of the story and relate them in the right order. She requires a little gentle prompting here and there when the pauses become particularly long. It is interesting to note that twice she directly ignores a question from her mother when she thinks it superfluous and it interrupts her train of thought. When she comes to the scene in the playground she becomes very animated and is obviously relishing the bully's come-uppance. She tends to pay great attention to detail which her sister apparently thinks unimportant; but, unlike Helen, she does not appear to have understood that the lion might return and she is, therefore, unconvinced by her own ending.

There is less difference in sentence construction than might have been expected, but there is predictably more repetition in Ruth's account than in Helen's. Both girls fail to point out that the lion was actually rather hungry, because he had had fish fingers for lunch when he would have preferred meat and he would have liked to eat Jack Tall, but refrained from doing so because he had promised not to eat anyone.

As each child told the story, it seemed that Helen was very well aware of the fantasy element in it and regarded the story with some amusement. Ruth, on the other hand, took it much more seriously and gave the impression that she half-believed it could happen.

THE ART OF CONVERSATION

It is often said that the art of conversation is a thing of the past and, if the emphasis is placed on the word 'art' this may well be true. What passes for conversation today is sometimes a series of dogmatic and intolerant assertions in which one speaker can hardly wait to interrupt another; but we must not generalize, for good conversation can still be heard and enjoyed.

Among the many generalizations by which we British are bedevilled is one that maintains that we are poor conversationalists. Now this is patently untrue of the Irish, for example. An inarticulate Irishman is rare, and conversation at almost all levels is free, wide-ranging and witty, albeit with a slight edge of malice. The Welsh are similarly fluent and indeed often positively poetical. Conversation in Scotland may take a graver tone but I have seldom found difficulty in conversing with the Scots; so this would seem to leave the unfortunate English alone on the defensive. A Canadian friend once complained to me that over a train journey of some three hundred miles no one in the carriage engaged in any kind of conversation. Why, he asked, were the *English* so God-damned stuffy! I explained as best I could that had he been in an Englishman's home he would have had little trouble, but that train travel is regarded as unpleasant enough without the risk of engaging in conversation with someone who might prove an unmitigated bore for the next five or six hours.

It is when one would *like* to communicate or to sustain a conversation which someone else has started, but cannot find the words, that it becomes a matter for concern.

Tadpoles grow into frogs in due course, so perhaps we should look at the 'tadpoles' of conversation first. We are taught to despise trivia but many a fruitful conversation has flourished after a seemingly trivial beginning. In fact, a light opening about the weather or the iniquities of a Sunday service that provides no refreshment on trains has the advantage of either opening the door to something more significant or of allowing the momentary contact to be broken easily and without embarrassment on either side if the 'option' is not taken up.

When it becomes apparent that both parties are prepared to enter into a conversation in a fuller sense, then the direction of the talk will usually fall to the more confident or better informed speaker. Thus, when the disparity between them is considerable it is a moral obligation on the part of the leader to find means of drawing out the less confident.

All of us must, at some time, have found ourselves trying to 'make conversation' with a shy or nervous guest who has found himself out of his depth and is hating every moment of it. When all our openings are ignored or countered with monosyllabic replies – door shutters like 'yes' and 'no' – then the going is hard indeed. But everyone has *something* which, once discovered, will arouse his interest. Those who have read that excellent book *A Kestrel For A Knave* by Barry Hines, or have seen the film of it, will recall the English master's surprise and pleasure in discovering that the almost illiterate and inarticulate boy, Billy Casper, could hold him and the class spellbound with his account of how to tame a kestrel. From a tentative beginning Billy warms into confidence and volubility and becomes, at times, almost lyrical on his secret hobby. The good conversationalist will put out patient feelers until he finds some vein of interest to bring an enthusiastic response. It always helps to word one's own conversation in such a way that – perhaps by inviting a direct opinion – an extended reply must seem the only possibility to the nervous speaker. Once such spontaneous communication has been achieved the initiator must settle down to be *a good and patient listener*.

It is a mistake, however, to believe that this or any other kind of conversation must roll on endlessly. Social conversation must be unforced. A companionable silence now and then gives space for fresh thought, a respite from concentration. The gushing type of earnest conversationalist who fears to stop for a moment is a great bore.

Until both parties are well acquainted it is also unwise to appear dogmatic or too argumentative. Only old and tried friends can afford to deride each other's opinions without causing offence. Never force the pace.

GROUP CONVERSATION

There is a marked resemblance in *good* group conversation to a professional football team, for the conversational 'ball' is passed neatly and unselfishly from one to another. The less able players will be in possession of the ball at some time but it is generally passed to the abler and more confident to make scoring points. The less able, with continuing practice, become in turn the scorers.

When one of the speakers becomes selfish and keeps the ball too much to himself, or the subject seems eternally glued to some side-issue, then a diversionary tactic is called for and this may be achieved by directly inviting an opinion from someone who seems excluded from the conversation. The thoughtful speaker will not be found wanting when such an occasion arises.

Awareness of the diversity of language and plenty of enjoyable practice in its social uses will prepare the future public speaker to surmount the next hurdle (often the most difficult) which is the careful dissimulation necessary in *formal* public speaking to appear calm, confident and even eager when one's most passionate desire is to slip out and go home while there is still time. Perhaps a comment from the irrepressible Falstaff may offer some comfort –

'Care I for the limb, the thews, the stature, bulk and big assemblance of a man! Give me the *spirit*.'

THE APPEARANCE OF CONFIDENCE

The fear of making a fool of oneself is probably the commonest disease known to mankind. It afflicts the beginner at golf, at dancing, at virtually every activity carried out in the presence of others; it causes the learner-driver to stall in the worst possible place and it undoubtedly causes the learner-speaker to 'stall' in the most public ones.

Nothing is easier – or less effective – than for the experienced to tell the nervous beginner 'not to worry'. Of *course* he will worry and, indeed, if he did not he would be either inhuman or insensitive.

We must first be clear about the nature of nervous tension if we are to make it an ally and not an enemy. Our nervous systems are so geared that, when danger seems imminent or any special physical effort is called for, all kinds of physiological changes occur in the blood-stream. Chemicals are created and rushed to various spots like reinforcements to an army. Muscles are tightened up preparatory to making a particularly violent effort. It is not necessary to understand the details, medically speaking. There is no virtue in the layman's knowing the Latin names. But it is necessary to understand that the end result – which we may loosely call 'stage-fright' – is not only a natural phenomenon but also a desirable one. We *should* be geared highly for the task before us. But – and this is the most essential thing to remember – we should have absolute control over the gears so that the change, as it were, may be smooth and may increase the power, not impede the movement.

It is a common sight in the wings of any theatre to see professional actors, before the curtain rises, performing curious little wriggling exercises, or rolling and twisting their hands and wrists to release the nervous tension which would otherwise cramp and spoil the freedom of their movements. These actors are nervous, sometimes extremely so; but once the curtain rises and they are in front of the public by whose favour they live, they are smoothly competent and apparently equally confident. They have *not lost their nervousness*; *they have harnessed and controlled it*, so that now it is their servant, bringing to their part more sparkle and power, not hampering the actor in any way.

Nervousness uncontrolled causes embarrassment not only to the performer but also to the listener and this, in turn, causes an unwilling dislike, for we do not care to be embarrassed and are apt to resent the person who makes us so. A painfully nervous and incompetent amateur actor who has to be prompted every third line causes the audience to feel a mixture of civilized pity and savage contempt because they are embarrassed by his incompetence and sorry for his obvious suffering. Only the chains of custom prevent them from crying aloud: 'For goodness sake, take him off.'

Now, the beginner in public speaking who is aware of his lack of confidence and consequent ineffectuality must first recognize the exact nature of his 'illness' and then set about resolutely curing himself, for, although others may advise and in this way assist, only he himself can effect an actual cure. After all, if he were to parade down the main shopping street of his town wearing some ludicrous garment he would expect to be laughed at. He would feel a fool because he looked one. It follows, therefore, that, in the simplest of psychological terms, we are apt to feel foolish if we look foolish, feel elegant if we look elegant, and feel confident if we look confident. The last statement is not, perhaps, quite as logical as it might seem because it is possible to look confident and be scared to death: but the important thing as far as the public performer is concerned is that, whatever his inner state his outward demeanour is all that concerns his audience and is what will colour their feelings towards him in the beginning at any rate.

Let's make a start. Look at yourself in a long mirror. Stand straight and stiff, like a soldier on parade. See how wooden it looks? This is the attitude of tension. Now place the feet comfortably apart, preferably with the left foot slightly in advance of the right and with the weight evenly divided between them. Smile at yourself. Now wriggle your shoulders as if you had hairs down your neck. Roll your head loosely round, keeping the body upright from the shoulders down. Swing the arms loosely like a rag-doll. *Think* the word 'loose' ... 'loose' ... 'LOOSE'. You are aiming to break down the nervous and muscular tension in your body and you must concentrate on what you are doing.

Now leave the mirror; go to the other side of the room. In a moment you are going to walk unhurriedly to the same spot you were in before, pause while you count two, smile pleasantly at your reflection and say: 'Good morning, Mrs Jones' (or whatever your own name is), turn and walk unhurriedly back to the door. Of course you will feel a fool and you will grin sheepishly at your own reflection. All right; don't let that worry you. It is getting rid of this 'I-felt-such-a-fool' complex that we are after. Ready? Now go.

Persevere with this exercise until you can do it without stiffness and without feeling that you are making an ass of yourself. However long it takes, keep at it. This is your first enemy: you must beat him unconditionally.

Now here is a simple announcement such as any of us might have to make; please read it carefully and then memorize it.

Ladies and gentlemen, before our guest-speaker tells us of his experiences in the Central Congo, he asks me to say that he would like you first to look at the specimens and photographs displayed in the lobby. The lecture will, therefore, begin a quarter of an hour later, at eight-fifteen.

In a moment you are going back in front of your mirror to make this announcement; you have only three things to remember: (1) the words, (2) you must not hurry, (3) you must not assume any 'special' voice. Ready? Go.

Now come back and let us think about this. First, read the announcement again. You see it falls into sections. First, the salutation 'Ladies and gentlemen', then a sentence ending with the word 'lobby', but itself divided into two natural parts, the dividing line falling on the word 'Congo'. This is where you would take a breath. Then there is a second sentence which could be taken comfortably on one breath; but which is better divided like the first, for a reason we will discuss in a moment.

First, the salutation. If you have to enter a room in which an audience is already seated, to make an announcement, you will find the audience busy with conversations and incidental noises. The greeting, 'Ladies and gentlemen', is their cue to pay attention to what is to follow; but you must give them grace; the noise needs several seconds to die; so, after you have 'saluted' them, you should pause for this purpose.

The announcement itself will fall into sentences or phrases separated by points at which you pause for breath. Your second task is to ensure that the tunes you play between these breathing points are not identical. In short, you now add music to words.

In drawing, a curved line is always more interesting than a straight one; and in speech straight lines are always to be avoided. They are monotonous. But sometimes speakers do play a tune that may even be quite pleasant. The trouble is that it is always the same tune. They repeat their melodic pattern: up, curve, down, down – up, curve, down, down! Pretty in its way, but always the same starting and finishing notes, which, although not a straight line, has the same monotonous effect.

Let us look again at the announcement. Having said: 'Ladies and gentlemen', and paused for attention, you now have a phrase to speak, beginning with 'before' and falling to a lower part of the voice-curve on the word 'Congo'. There is then a breathing point. Now begins a longer curve ending the phrase *and* the sentence, on the word 'lobby'. Remember that your voice should reach a lower note on 'lobby' than it did on 'Congo', not only to mark the end of the sentence; but to avoid repeating the tune you sang in the first phrase.

Say just that much first, concentrating on these points.

Now back to the announcement. This time we will finish it.

We are left with a statement and a reminder. The statement is simply that the lecture will begin a quarter of an hour later; and the reminder is the phrase which tells the audience that this will be at eight-fifteen. It is a small courtesy which saves the audience from working out the revised time for themselves.

Next we have to consider the 'tune' for this phrase. We do not have to be difficult about this. If the tune for this phrase is almost the same as that for the first, we need not quibble. An over-stressed tune becomes singing rather than speaking; but there is one point to watch. The voice should not descend too low before the final phrase. This is because the note upon which we say the word 'fifteen' must be emphatically low by contrast with the note sounded previously. If the speaker neglects this emphasis, the audience is not aware that the last word has been sounded, and waits for something else to be said. The last (*low*) note is the vocal full stop.

Now walk calmly back before your mirror and make the whole announcement unhurriedly, bringing out all the points that have been emphasized. If you think too much fuss has been made about a few simple lines, repeat the entire announcement quickly and on one note. The contrast will speak for itself.

When you are sure of this exercise vary it by making up a few similar exercises for yourself. Do not be too serious, and concentrate on making both the voice *and* the face express your meaning. More will be said about facial expression later: just now remember to look alert and interested in what you are saying.

When you can tackle any short announcement of this kind easily you will have learned the art of looking confident. You will be able to make an embryonic speech without looking or feeling foolish, and without embarrassing your audience.

BUILDING UP A SHORT SPEECH

Now here are a number of terse statements out of which you are to build up a brief but pleasant speech, arranging them in the most effective order, and enlarging each without undue padding. The first has been done for you as an example:

The Main Facts –

Harvest Supper, Saturday, September 23rd at 8 pm.

Principal Speaker – James Harding Esq., Secretary National Federation of Church Clubs.

Proceeds in aid of fund to provide furniture for the Youth Club Chapel.

The Speech –

Ladies and gentlemen,

Our Youth Club, now in its ninth year, has been making a wonderful contribution to the work of the Church in many ways. The Club premises have grown, by the efforts of the members, from one room in a prefabricated hut, to five rooms in the Church Annexe; and most of you will have seen the new reading-room which the boys and girls have recently decorated so well in their spare time.

Now, thanks to the generosity of one of our Councillors, the Club has acquired a fine hut at the rear of the Annexe for use as a private chapel. The members are now busily painting and decorating this; but furniture is needed, too, and this is beyond the resources of the Club funds. The Church Council has decided, therefore, that for this year the proceeds of the Harvest Supper will be given entirely to the Youth Club for the purchase of chapel furniture.

For this reason I appeal to you now to make a special effort to support the Harvest Supper, not only by your own attendance, but by bringing along your friends too, so that we shall be able to raise enough money for this excellent purpose.

The principal speaker at the Supper this year will be Mr James Harding, the popular secretary of the National Federation of Church Clubs, and the Supper will be on

Saturday, September 23rd at 8 pm. The tickets are on sale now. I hope that you will buy them and mark the date in your diaries for your special attention.

In the order of presentation the name of the principal speaker was left to the end, as this was of lesser importance than the reason for his appearance; and the date and time were put last because the audience would wish to make a note of them; and would not care to interrupt the speaker in the middle of his speech to do so. Simple speeches of this kind are ideal to use for practice in speech-building. You need not worry about being clever or brilliantly humorous. All you are required to do is to get over a few facts clearly and pleasantly, practising relaxation and poise as you do so.

Now here are three sets of facts. See if you can work them up into three pleasant little speeches on the lines you have just been shown.

1. The Course in Beginner's Oil Painting opens after dinner this evening, at about 7.45 pm.

2. There will be an address of welcome by the Warden, Sir Thomas Wayne-Margin, in the library.

3. The first lecture, on MAKING A START IN ART, will be given by Mr James Hunter Mearing, RA, at 8 pm.

4. During the week-end there will be painting exercises in the Abbey grounds, weather permitting. If wet other arrangements will be made.

5. Art materials may be bought from the Store, which is open between 9–11 am and 2–4 pm.

6. The Course ends after lunch on Sunday. Transport to the station will be available up to 4 pm.

7. The Warden and Staff hope all students will enjoy the Course and find it useful.

1. The Pengrayling Women's Institute – announcement at ordinary evening session.

Some members have been complaining that the weekly meetings are dull and the programmes unenterprising.

2. The Committee is worried about this and anxious to improve the situation if it can.

3. The Committee invites suggestions from members as to how the programmes could be improved.

4. Regarding guest speakers, members should bear in mind that good speakers are generally expensive. When expenses are added to a speaker's fees, it makes a great strain on the Institute's funds.

5. The Drama section is in urgent need of members; if these were forthcoming, we should have more home-made entertainment at least.

1. Annual General Meeting of the Trinchooma Development Company.

The Directors apologize for the delay in starting the meeting.

2. We have just had word that the Chairman had a slight motoring accident on his way here and was taken to hospital for minor attention. He is expected to be here in about half an hour.

3. Coffee will be brought round in a few minutes.

4. The police say that a Humber car, No BCU 51560, parked near the corner of Branton Street, is causing some obstruction. Will the owner please move it?

5. We much regret the inconvenience caused by this delay.

INTRODUCING A SPEAKER

These exercises have been confined to very simple material on the basis of known facts. Now, to take a logical step forward, let us try introducing another speaker. Here we are still dealing with known facts, but their presentation is more difficult. The aim is two-fold – to explain to the audience who and what the speaker is, and to make the man himself feel welcome. It is, at the same time, an exercise in economy, because your concern is to say just as much as will do this but no more. It is irritating and in bad taste to set out to introduce a speaker and then trespass on his time and your hearers' patience, by giving them your own views. They have come to hear him and will welcome you only as a short and necessary link between the speaker and themselves.

Here is an example. The speaker is Colonel Lloyd-Pugh, VC, DSO. The occasion is a meeting of a local Regimental Association of which you are Chairman. You rise to introduce the speaker in the following terms:

Members and friends,

We have been fortunate in getting for our guest-speaker tonight Colonel David Lloyd-Pugh, VC, DSO; and I am honoured in being permitted to introduce to you one of the most famous holders of the Victoria Cross in this country.

Colonel Lloyd-Pugh was the raiser and first commander of 'X' Commando in the last war. He welded an originally small number of – in his own words – military oddities and individualists into a most deadly and respected fighting force which slew and harassed the enemy on many 'cloak and dagger' raids with unremitting venom. Of these men it was said by the Prime Minister that they left a trail of German corpses between them and the shore.

Under its inspired leader the Commando made the green beret the most coveted headgear among the cream of Britain's fighting men; and it will be our privilege this evening to hear more, from Colonel Lloyd-Pugh himself, of this proud and historic force.

So, without more ado, I will ask him to speak to us now.

Ladies and gentlemen . . . Colonel Lloyd-Pugh.

You may care to invent similar introductory speeches for one or all of the following:

(a) A distinguished politician.
(b) A great scientist.
(c) A famous test-pilot.
(d) A doctor from a famous leper-colony.

(*e*) A leading couturier.

(*f*) A famous composer of light-opera.

(*g*) A famous actor or actress.

(*h*) A famous film-star.

(*i*) A leading member of Scotland Yard.

An introductory speech of this kind should never take more than three or four minutes. If you can't do justice to the character you are about to introduce in this time, you should let someone else handle the business for you.

EXTENDED NARRATIVE

The next step from here is to lengthen the duration of your speech while retaining its nature. We are all interested in each other, and it will be excellent to give a short biographical talk on some famous person, living or dead.

This will require a little more skill. There is a danger that the speaker may not select his material very well and may dwell unduly on unimportant details of the subject's life, at the expense of more interesting and vital narrative. The audience will want to know what kind of man the subject was and what his contribution was to the sum of human experience. The narrative must have enough detail and always be coloured with human interest. Let us take Ludwig van Beethoven for an example.

Here was one of the greatest musical geniuses the world will ever know who, towards the end of his life, composed and played incomparable music of which he could not hear one note. This in itself is wonderful. But Beethoven's whole life was a masterpiece of surmounted difficulties.

He was born of a Flemish family in 1770 and spent a poverty-stricken childhood. The 'van' had no aristocratic significance. His mother, to whom he gave unstinted affection, was the daughter of a cook, his father a worthless tippler in service as a singer to the Elector of Cologne. His childhood was hard and unnatural, for his father, in sober moments, perceived musical genius in his son and drove him remorselessly to fashion him into an infant prodigy out of which to make more money for drink. In this he failed.

By the time he was seventeen Beethoven's mother had died and the besotted widower having sold every stick in the house for drink, Ludwig became actual if not nominal head of the family, his father being beyond any practical assistance. He had two younger brothers and had to work as a piano tutor for miserable fees in order to support them and his father.

Fortune, however, was with the young man, for he came into contact with a wealthy and cultured family, the Van Breunings of Cologne, to whose children he became tutor.

The Van Breunings could recognize genius when they saw it; and in this surly, scowling, roughly-spoken youngster, with his curly hair and fierce blue eyes, they saw not only musical genius but a deep and stubborn loneliness, for the young Beethoven had had no fun out of his short life, and had never come into contact with cultured thought in any direction.

Soon, under their kindly influence, Ludwig blossomed out in every direction. He learned the joys of literature and cultured interests and he experienced the healing power of a happy family life, for the Van Breunings were sincerely fond of him and he became almost an adopted son.

From Van Breuning he was given an introduction to the great Count Waldstein – to whom he was later to dedicate one of his most famous piano works – and through him he went to Vienna with letters of introduction to those who could further his musical career.

Soon his genuis poured itself out in a flood of the mightiest music the world had yet heard. Symphonies, concertos, quartets, serenades, pieces for every instrument and songs, flowed unceasingly in this torrent of creation. The humble lad of peasant origin was fêted on all sides; but even as he stood almost on the pinnacle of success, the seeds of tragedy were germinating in him. He was becoming deaf.

Although settling deeper and deeper into despair and the

terrible loneliness of the deaf, Beethoven never ceased to compose and, between partial and complete deafness, he wrote, among other great works, the Eroica Symphony, probably his most magnificent creation. By 1802 he was stone-deaf, and yet for the next eleven years he poured out superb works, including his three greatest piano works: the Waldstein, in honour of his old friend and patron, the Appassionata and the majestic Emperor concerto. In this period, too, he composed his fifth symphony, the opening bars of which were later to become the famous 'V for Victory' motif that swept occupied Europe just before the liberation.

Now in spite of fame and comfortable means Beethoven was plunged to the depths of unhappiness by his affliction. His deafness could not cut him off from the sources of his musical genius, for he heard the notes in his head; but it deprived him of human comfort and friendship. In 1824 he visited London and, with the London Philharmonic Society, he conducted his last two great works—the Solemn Mass and the mighty Ninth Symphony. Poor Beethoven could hear neither the music nor the tumultuous applause with which it was greeted. Already death was nibbling at the stubborn frame that had resisted the assaults of poverty and want. He was suffering from a progressive disease of the liver which, on March 26th, 1827, finally stopped the flow of his genius and left Music in mourning for her greatest son.

This kind of 'potted' biography makes good material for short lectures, and its preparation makes a demand on the ability to separate important points from trivialities.

Why not try your hand at a similar short lecture on the life of some great person? If you want some suggestions to be going on with, here are a few to consider:

Father Damien, Dr Albert Schweitzer, Benjamin Disraeli, Christopher Marlowe, Albert Einstein, Jacob Epstein, Sir Harry Lauder, Samuel Pepys, Dr Samuel Johnson, Dr Harvey Crippen.

You will find your local Reference Library useful here. Public speakers should be accustomed to ferreting out facts and assimilating them.

THINKING ABOUT YOUR SPEECH

We have all known the experience of going to bed completely foxed by some problem, only to find, in the morning, the right answer ready-made, worked out for us by our subconscious mind while we slept. A public speech is based on a firm foundation when there has been a good deal of subconscious thought around it first.

It is a good mental discipline to make the mind concentrate on a definite line of thought even when no immediate action is to follow. There are moments in every day when the mind is in neutral gear. When one is shaving or doing something equally mechanical the mind is usually occupied with a kind of mental hedge-hopping, vague thought leading to no real conclusion. These are moments when the outline of a speech can be sketched in by encouraging the mind to think *round* the subject. You will find then that the ideas will fall more tidily into place when full concentration is given to it, because a certain amount of subconscious foundation has been laid.

THINKING ABOUT BASIC PRINCIPLES

Although our principles are the ideals for which we are most likely to die if need be, they are, paradoxically, the ideas about which we are often most hazy. We often say that something is against our principles or refer to it as a matter of principle; but on being pinned down, we often find it difficult to explain exactly what we do mean by principles.

Now public speakers often speak on matters of conscience —which are matters of principle—and political speakers particularly are apt to talk very glibly on these lines; and it is important that they should be certain what they mean, for if they don't know what they mean themselves, there is small chance of their knowing what the other fellow means either.

Principles, you see, are abstractions, and abstractions are difficult to equate. I suggest you examine the following list of abstract nouns and try to define with absolute clarity what *you* mean when you speak of them.

tyranny	liberty	freedom
equality	education	responsibility
virtue	faith	superstition
honesty	justice	truth
morality	conscience	class (social)
reaction	democracy	good citizenship

In the course of your speech-making you will dwell, sooner or later, on some or all of these concepts, and the more they figure in your conscious thought now the more explicit will be your conversations about them.

Thought of this kind is an essential part of good speech-building; the public speaker should not be bound within narrow limits: the wider his field of thought the more interesting he is likely to prove to others. Later, when dealing with debate and private argument, we shall see some of the traps that gape for the 'foggy' thinker. It does not follow, we should remember, that because we mean a certain thing when we speak of, say, faith, that our neighbour means the same when he does.

BUILDING UP A POLITICAL SPEECH

It is not uncommon to hear: 'Politicians! They're *all* a pack of liars; wouldn't trust one of 'em: out for their own ends, the lot of them,' though the people who say this kind of thing generally vote for *someone* just the same. However, the professional politician is always rather suspect in this country. If he is a failure he is derided, and if a success he is likely to be called an 'opportunist'.

There are certain individuals who, by colourful and flamboyant oratory, have become famous; but they are a tiny minority among the many who speak in political circles daily. Most speakers have to be content with less exotic speech, which is just as well, for one can have too much of anything.

We are all politicians in an amateur way, and in our more expansive moments are pretty sure we could put the whole business of government straight, or at any rate straighter than that ass So-and-so seems to be doing!

Party government has docketed us all more or less tidily on the left, right, or in the middle; but there are always many citizens who, either because of indifference or self-interest, vacillate from one direction to another. This electoral 'flotsam' provides fine hunting material for the party politician.

Now, supposing you to be engaged in local politics on one side or another, how should you set about (a) capturing the floating voter, and (b) converting from the ranks of your opponents?

To begin with, abusive derogation is not a good idea. You may influence your hearers at the time with a piece of colourful slanging of the other side; but when the impact of your personality is no longer apparent sober reflection is likely to cancel out much of the initial effect. To put over your party view really effectively you should:

(a) Be absolutely clear what your line is and be able to explain it in simple terms to any kind of audience.

(b) Be equally clear about your opponent's line. You can't refute an argument if you don't know what it is.

(c) Be aware of what aspects of national and international affairs are, at the time, most important and do not waste your time and your hearers' patience on trivialities.

(d) Leave your audience with the conviction (if only grudgingly held) that you know where you are going and why, and that you would make a pleasant travelling companion!

Political speakers have most temptation to be, or seem to be, pompous. Great care should be taken not to use hackneyed or self-satisfied phrases that really mean nothing. These are the sterile paddings used by political speakers when they have nothing to say, but wish to conceal the fact. Such phrases as 'the ship of State' and 'the strong hand on the helm' brand the speaker as a pompous ass. They rank with 'the white man's burden' as objects of derision.

Now, for practice, prepare a short speech on *your* party's policy on some or all of the following points:

(*a*) Should we have industrial incentives?
(*b*) Alliance with USA on Middle East policy.
(*c*) The future of the UNO as far as Britain's relations with it are concerned.
(*d*) Old Age Pensioners.
(*e*) Housing.
(*f*) Education.
(*g*) Military Service.
(*h*) Inflationary tendencies.

The television service has shown us party political discussions in which a speaker on one side has writhed around impatiently in his chair, pulling faces and sighing contemptuously while his opponent put his views. This kind of behaviour, apart from being extremely rude, is childishly ineffective, because it is plain bad psychology to infer that everyone who disagrees with you is a moron. We may be persuaded by logic and emotional colouring to adopt someone else's viewpoint; but we are hardly likely to fly into the arms of anyone who plainly thinks us fools for the views we hold.

Now, suppose *you* are to make a political speech at a local meeting of 'X' Party. What should you do, in practical terms, to prepare your speech?

First, decide which aspect of foreign or domestic affairs is most important just now, and learn your party's policy on it *thoroughly*. Find out also what the attitude of your party has been to this question *in the past* and what action was then taken. Choose those topics which will be most effective and concentrate on them. Do not diffuse your speech by trying to cover too many aspects at once.

Now arrange the points you have selected in the order of their importance, making sure that the final point shall be a brief – and memorable – summary of the speech as a whole.

Next consider what your opponents have said and done on these issues in the past. Have they made definite promises concerning them? If so, have they kept them? Do not attempt to discredit your opponents unless you can quote – *accurately* – facts and figures in support of your accusation.

Remember that you will be more effective in proportion to the *positiveness* of your speech. Never apologize for your Party. Merely to prove that you have never done any harm is no proof that you have ever done any good. It is better to spend time explaining what your party has done and will do, rather than waste it in explaining what your opponents have *not* done.

When you have done this, examine your speech carefully for contradictions and inaccuracies, and especially for padding. Never let your words stand in the way of your meaning. Words should always clarify, never obstruct. If you prune mercilessly you will be surprised to find how few words are necessary to explain your views and how much better your speech is for this. The question of economy is dealt with in greater detail later. For the moment it will be enough to keep everything simple and not to strive for effect with over-dressed language.

You will find it useful to cut out reports of the more important speeches made by all sides in Parliament and file them for future reference. The political 'tune' changes surprisingly over the course of the years, and many a politician has been embarrassed to be reminded of what he said on a previous occasion!

Try always to analyse the speeches of other speakers and

know their strong points and their weaknesses. It will help you greatly with the composition of your own speeches later.

'HOW' IS MORE IMPORTANT THAN 'WHAT'

Although examples are given here and there, the main purpose of this book is to advise you on *how* to compose and deliver a speech rather than on what to say. There are many excellent books published on the formulae of public speaking; these will tell you the formal wording for particular occasions, will differentiate between the duties of chairman, secretary, treasurer, and the like. They should be consulted when you are uncertain of such things; but it is vital that you should become as expert as possible in putting it over before you become too involved with formalities. Never neglect any opportunity to learn and practise more of the art of *living* speech. You can teach a parrot to imitate expertly, but you cannot teach him to colour and interpret words. *The most correct and beautifully articulated speech is useless without colour and vitality.*

The earnest beginner should study any and every kind of speech, from the streets around him, from the pulpit, the theatre, the political cockpit – anywhere. He should neglect no source of study that can enrich his own experience, and he should make analysis a habit.

He should not only be aware of an effect, but of how it has been produced.

There is a place for the 'Example'. Books are published from which you can copy specimens of letters for all occasions. These are undeniably useful; but we should not mistake their limitations. Suppose I want to write a love-letter to a girl who is intelligent enough to spot mechanical passion when she reads it! What then? By all means look at examples now and then, but only by making up your own speeches and learning from your earlier mistakes can you become an effective public speaker. The speech must not only be yours, it must be YOU. That is, it should not be a pale reflection of what someone else has advised you to say; it should be an extension of your own personality. Don't worry if it is faulty here and there. I cannot learn to write like Shakespeare simply because I revere his works. It is fairly certain that your speech is a great deal better than you think it is, and it is a *natural, healthy product,* not a sickly imitation. NEVER BE AFRAID TO BE YOURSELF.

I read somewhere during the war about a nervous young Naval Lieutenant detailed to lecture to an audience of senior officers on some technical development concerning radar. He looked down at the sea of gold braid, licked his lips and, taking his courage in his hands, began: 'Gentlemen, there are many people who know more about this subject than I . . . (pause) . . . but, *as I don't see any of them present,* I will begin — '

DOING WITHOUT PROPS

In one way or another we spend much of our lives learning to be independent of props. The baby held up by his mother soon learns to do without the supporting hand, the boy learning to ride a bicycle learns to balance alone, and so on. Have you ever watched a nervous amateur in his first part? As sure as there is a chair on the stage or a settee, he will cling to the back of it as he speaks. He needs a prop to bolster up his confidence. The public speaker is similiarly affected by nerves. Think for a moment of the props you have seen speakers use. Have you included these?

> Chairbacks for leaning on.
> Coins for jingling.
> Keys for playing with.
> Spectacles for polishing.
> Handkerchiefs for nose-polishing.
> Notes for folding.
> Wineglasses for twisting.
> Cigarettes for crumbling.

I am sure you can think of many more. This is a weakness that simply has to be fought. We all have it; none of us can afford to be superior. First, ask a friend to tell you honestly what mannerisms and fidgety habits you possess; then set about eliminating them. Concentrate on just ... standing ... *still*. It is one of the hardest things to do; the bugbear of every young actor: but this quality of repose, once you have attained it, will lift you from the ranks of the mediocre to those of the respected; then the road is clear for further improvement.

A speaker standing still (not stiff) and looking self-possessed is a long way on the path to success because he has laid a good foundation. The audience can concentrate on what he is saying because they are not distracted by irrelevant antics. The best way to practise doing without these props is to surround yourself with them, give yourself every opportunity, like a man determined to stop smoking, who puts a box within reach and sneers at himself every time his hand strays in that direction. Put a chair where you can lean on it, and a table where you can both lean or squat on it, covered with the most delightful objects for playing with, and REFUSE TO DO ANY OF THESE THINGS.

USING THE FACE AND THE EYES

There is a school of thought which holds that facial expression is a kind of indecency, un-British, all right for foreigners don't-you-know, but simply not done at home. You may think this attitude is confined to the few remaining specimens of Colonel Blimp, but unfortunately that is not so. It is much more common than you would suppose, though it is not, perhaps, so frankly expressed. Let us examine the idea objectively for a moment.

To start with, I suggest you switch on the television when there is either a play or a political argument on the bill, and then turn off the sound. Now watch the faces carefully. The man on the left is angry; how do you know? 'Why, I can see it on his face,' you reply. Similarly, you can see when he is amused, contemptuous, about to make a decision, hurt, afraid, bewildered, sleepy, and so on. *You can see it on his face.* These are British players. If they were French you would see these emotions even more clearly, for the vitality of French playing makes it a most exciting experience. You will also think some of the faces the people make are too funny for words, but don't laugh too long, because you and I look like that, as well, when we are 'wound up'!

This is your answer to the 'stiff-upper-lip-old-boy' school of thought which really should have passed decently away by now. *A 'deadpan' is an invitation to inattention.* If you don't look interested in what you are saying you cannot expect your audience to take an interest either.

The frozen face, to be fair, is more often a result of fright than a desire to be impassive. It is a natural offspring of embarrassment, but an audience is not to know this. They may easily mistake it for (*a*) superiority or (*b*) boredom.

It is possible to appear to be looking directly at someone without actually meeting their eye, and this is a wise thing to practise. You see, if you gaze hard at the ceiling, as some nervous speakers do, you displace the focus of attention, which should be on you, but is not, because it has followed the direction of your gaze. Appear to look directly at the people you are addressing. You need not focus too sharply on them.

Also, do not neglect any section of the audience. It is easy to make your remarks almost entirely to one side of the room or to the middle of the audience. If you were in one of the neglected sections you would feel hurt or indignant. After all, you have paid your money too!

The fixed stare at some unfortunate individual is also a mistake. Speakers do this sometimes, and it causes great perturbation to the individual singled out (so he thinks) for your undivided attention. You aren't really looking at him, just using him as a convenient focal point: but he doesn't know that and may well fear that there is something alarmingly wrong with his appearance, poor chap.

SPEAKING 'OFF THE CUFF'

The Americans say they are speaking 'off the cuff' when they are doing so with little or no warning; and this may be your first public speech. We are all, sooner or later, called on at some social affair to 'say a few words'. This is a phrase which almost paralyses some people, so that they are only able to mumble a sentence or two and sit down, their evening ruined.

There are two main reasons for this. The first is that they do not know what is expected of them, and the second that they cannot think of anything to say.

Many people think that 'say a few words' means 'rise and give an exhibition of high-powered oratory'. Nothing could be further from the truth. It means exactly what it says. A few simple friendly words. No more. Neither are you expected to be particularly witty. These are occasions for homespun oratory. Don't misunderstand this. It does not mean careless or crude speaking. It just means simple thoughts simply expressed with brevity and good humour. You are not expected to be 'clever' or sensational. You are expected to be a 'nice' person acting 'nicely'. There will be occasions when you *will* be expected to display oratorical skill and humour with a polish; but not now.

'But what do I say?' you ask. All right. Let's discuss that. First of all an axiom. You cannot speak fluently without ideas. Granted that this is so, you then have to look for a source of ideas to talk about. Go out to the newsagent and buy a few magazines and newspapers – start with the popular weeklies such as *Woman's Own* and a couple of newspapers such as the *Daily Express* and the *Daily Herald*. Turn to the pages which contain 'Letters To The Editor', and there is your first – and one of your most fertile fields of material, because *these letters have not been written by experts*, but by ordinary people like ourselves. They give a fair cross-section of public opinion on a wide range of subjects, expressed in plain language. Let's look at one –

Can nothing be done to stop the organized 'begging' that is carried on nearly every Saturday under the guise of a flag day? The whole principle of flag days should be investigated. Extracting money from the public is both irritating and undignified.

M.H.O. Reading.

Now consider this letter for a moment. It doesn't matter whether you agree with it or not. If you want fluent ideas, then you must not come to an immediate conclusion, because there are numerous ideas arising from this point. First, think of the objects of such charity – cancer relief, care of children, care of the blind, care of war-cripples, care of spastics, the Red Cross, and many others. Are these, in your opinion, worthy charities? Could the money be raised any other way? Appeals in the Press, on the wireless or television, or raised by direct taxation; if the latter, how would it be imposed to ensure that no one dodged his responsibility? Is it true to say that asking for contributions for such causes is undignified? What do the collectors get out of it? Are the blind and the maimed and diseased grateful for what is done? Is goodness in itself sufficient reward? You will agree, I hope, that there is sufficient matter here for quite a lot of discussion, and there is much more that could be said. Let us put the next point on a line by itself because it is important.

Ideas Breed Ideas

The more you come into contact with the ideas of other people, whether they are interesting or dull, bigoted or casual, clever or stupid, the more your own ideas will multiply, and the more you will have to talk about.

Let us take another letter.

Now that women are on equal terms with men in almost all walks of life, why have men still got the monopoly of the pulpit. Women are as well – and better – able to preach God's word as men. Must the male sex always claim superiority in morals as well as everything else?

Pro Femina. Leeds.

Pro Femina is a little weak on grammar, but forthright enough on his subject. 'He' may be a woman, but let us assume that he is masculine. Admirers of Dr Johnson will recall the classic answer to this question: 'Sir, a woman preaching is like a dog walking on his hind legs. It is not well done, but you are surprised to find it done at all.' But our aim is not to dispose of the question in this masterly fashion, but to use it as a fertilizer for fresh ideas.

It may help to buy a cheap pocket-book, cut out this letter and stick it on a left-hand page. On the opposite page jot down in précis form *all* the ideas that come to you in whatever order they come. Think until you have bled the question dry. Then you may like to revise your jottings, get them in sequence, keeping together things that should be thought of together, cutting out repetitions and unnecessary phrases and generally tidying up. You will be astonished to find how much material you can produce from this small root.

A notebook is as necessary to a public speaker or writer as it is to a policeman. Thought is a fugitive creature and is best pinned down at birth.

It is by contantly mulling over other people's
ideas that we can strengthen and focus our own:

The great advantage of a small book like this is that you can study it unobtrusively almost anywhere. There you are in a train or café, apparently reading; but actually busy composing speeches in your head. It is excellent practice and passes time more usefully than snoozing!

VENTURING INTO THE BATTLEFIELD

A battlefield presupposes an enemy; but the public speaker should not regard his audience in this light. Except for certain political occasions, audiences are neutral, waiting for *you* to put them into gear. No, the enemy is the 'gremlin' perching on your shoulder and whispering in your ear:

'You look a fearful fool; what do you know about this subject anyhow; and whatever made you think you could speak in public? They're laughing at you in the back row,' he adds.

Learn to recognize this little fiend for what he is, a cunning and implacable menace, creeping up with fine impartiality on kings and commoners, preachers, politicians, salesmen and teachers – and ordinary bodies like you and me.

Let us look in at the Village Hall for a moment, where a packed house is waiting to hear the Squire, Sir Reginald Roose-Ribald, MC, JP, address them on behalf of the Ratepayers' Association, which disapproves of the extravagance of the Much Millyng Council. Mr Cyril Meanwell, a local government clerk, new to the game and terrified of Sir Reginald and the audience, rises to introduce the speaker.

'Er . . . Ladies and . . . er . . . Gentlemen,' begins Mr Meanwell. Then, feeling that more warmth might be looked for, he adds, 'Friends and . . . er . . . fellow, er . . . fellow . . . ratepayers. I know you don't want to hear . . . er . . . that is . . . from me.' This is a fatal opening. They were not very keen on him to start with; but now he has put the idea into their heads they quite see his point! 'So I'm only going to say a few words.' (This cliché has come to mean 'I now propose to drool away for hours and you try stopping me,' so that, at best, it can only be greeted with polite disbelief.)

At this point Mr Meanwell has completed a series of leg-movements beginning with fifth position and ending with legs crossed; he has now adopted what can only be described as 'a Henry VIII' with his toes turned in. This is convulsing a gaggle of girls in the front row, and has caused Mr Meanwell to turn a shade of red more in keeping with the character he is about to introduce. The incarceration of his hands, which have been thrust deep in his jacket pockets, worries Mr Meanwell, so he removes them and adopts a prima-donna bosom-clasp that brings the girls to the verge of hysterics and almost completes the speaker's demoralization. Gazing glassily over the heads of the girls, and speaking in a strained falsetto, Mr Meanwell continues: 'You all know our speaker, Sir Reginald Roose-Ribald, and no introduction is necessary from me. Indeed, it would really be an impertinence, ha, ha!' By now the fluency of one who has no more to lose has descended on the unfortunate Meanwell, and he embarks on an outline of Sir Reginald's life and services to the community that includes every committee he ever served on and does not even despise the Presidency of the Pig Club. And all to the accompaniment of such a gallery of balletic movements, head-noddings, bleatings, and 'er's and 'ah's that the audience, fascinated by his antics, has barely heard, and certainly not attended to, a word he has said.

We laugh at poor Meanwell because he is funny and doesn't want to be; he has clown pathos: but we are not involved, just looking on. If we were seriously concerned with the subject of the meeting, and felt that Sir Reginald had something important to say about it, Mr Meanwell would not amuse us. On the contrary, we should be rough with him. 'Why doesn't the fool shut up and sit down?' we would snarl.

The Meanwells of this world are adult people who have had to learn many other skills to keep their self-respect in the community; they could learn this skill, too, if they tried. Let us not be too soft with them.

The man who would not think for a moment that he could play the piano without first learning what the notes meant, is strangely blind about public speaking. It does not occur to him that this, too, is a skill and has to be learned the hard way. Even knowing what you want to say is not enough. You must learn the technique of 'putting it over'.

It will be as well to try first a speech of the more semi-formal kind that will not make too many demands on us.

Let us turn back for a moment to the answer to 'what is expected of me?' *Simple thoughts, simply expressed with brevity and good humour*. What about an office presentation? Let's set the scene.

We are in the office of a grain-and-seed merchant. The

manager is about to present a golf-bag to Mr Edward Harper, who, at sixty-six, is retiring after forty-odd years with the firm, rising from clerk to accountant. The staff are grouped round the room in attitudes of self-conscious attention. Tea and chocolate biscuits have been handed round to relieve the tension. Mr Harper, also looking uncomfortable, is sitting stiffly near the window. The manager, wearing an air of assumed ease and good-fellowship, and clutching an envelope upon which he has jotted down 'a few ideas', is standing in the middle of the 'stage'. There is the scene; up with the curtain.

Frowning at the office-boy who is helping himself rather lavishly to biscuits, and clearing his throat noisily, the manager speaks. 'Well,' he says, '*tempus fugit*, you know; we'd better get on with the business of the day, ha, ha, ha; I'm sorry to say, that is, we all are, ha, ha, I feel sure. Well, friends, we all know why we're here. All good things must come to an end, they say; though we hope Mr Harper, "Ted", I should say . . . you won't mind me calling you Ted before all these young people on this day, I am sure . . . where was I? Yes, Ted's leaving us, as we know, and it's been a long time – how many years is it, Ted? Forty-three! Well, well! I must say you'd never think it, to look at him. You wouldn't, you know, Ted. Would you, friends? Of course he started young, didn't you, Ted? I hope I look as fit when I'm your . . . Ted started here as a clerk, you know. Just like you, Mr Hopkins, only he worked harder. And now he's leaving us, and we have a little surprise for him (he's been standing with a brand-new golf-bag just behind him for the last half-hour!), and we hope he'll like it and that the exercise will keep him fit for many a long day. And it's *been* a long day; I know. I've been here thirty-five years myself. It's changed a lot, though, has the old firm. The Guv'nor when I came was a terror, wasn't he, Ted? You wouldn't remember him, of course (this to the rest of the staff); but he was. I remember . . .'

We don't need to follow this speech any further, do we? 'Ted' gets his golf-bag in the end; and by that time he's earned it! The point is that if you have paid attention to the advice given earlier in this book you will not 'wiffle' like this. You will say what is necessary with as much sincerity, in a third of the time and much more tidily.

It takes practice to develop the ability to wrap your words up neatly. Let us work out a better speech for the office manager to have made. First of all, he should have avoided saying: 'We all know why we are here.' Statements of the obvious such as this give your speech a haphazard sound at once. He should have called his colleague '*Mr* Harper' until the extreme end, because it is unwise to use Christian names with older employees in the presence of very young ones and takes too much of the ceremony out of the occasion. After all, it *is* an occasion, and, while not wanting to make it coldly formal, it should be marked by enough ceremony to show Mr Harper that his services have been valued.

Having embarked on his speech, the manager should have stuck to the point, and not strayed into reminscences that could have been familiar to Mr Harper and to no one else.

All speeches have 'a line', and this line should be followed through to the end. The purpose of the gathering we are discussing is twofold – to show the retiring accountant that we are sorry to lose his company; and to present him with a golf-bag to mark the occasion. This is our 'line' and it should be a straight one.

The use of the Christian name *once* at the end of the speech stresses the personal warmth of feeling on the manager's side. 'Goodbye, Ted, and ... (shaking hands) ... good luck.' The manager's speech might have taken the following form:

> Mr Harper, ladies and gentlemen, anyone can see that this is a special occasion, for, apart from the chocolate biscuits and the presence of a brand-new golf-bag among the furnishings, I am speaking and all my staff are paying respectful attention to me at once!
>
> We are here to present this golf-bag to Mr Harper as a

gesture of respect and affection on his retirement; and we have first to say goodbye to a colleague we are sincerely sorry to lose, and whose company we shall miss.

Mr Harper has been with this firm for many years. Even those of us who have worked with Mr Harper for only a short time, however, will have found him a good friend and colleague, slow to blame and quick to encourage. To me, particularly, he has been a most loyal friend and assistant.

We are not, however, going to say goodbye too sadly. Mr Harper is not going to stagger through the years of his retirement; he is a strong and vigorous golfer, as I know to my cost, and a man of many hobbies and interests. He is going to *enjoy* every minute of his retirement; and I hope we can help him in some small way.

It is traditional, I believe, to present retiring colleagues with a clock – it has always seemed singularly inept to me – but *we* are not going to do so. Mr Harper doesn't consult time very much, he *uses* it: so we have decided to present him instead with a means to that end, and we hope he will applaud the decision.

Mr Harper, you (very sensibly) are not sorry to retire; and we are not sorry for you, only for ourselves in losing your company. We shall miss each other in many ways, I know. Now, on behalf of the staff and myself, I ask you to accept this golf-bag to mark the esteem and affection in which we hold you. Goodbye, Ted . . . and good luck!

It would be a helpful exercise to write out an alternative speech that you might have made in the circumstances.

CHRISTIAN-NAME TERMS

Opinion is sharply divided on the use of Christian names between speakers on public occasions. Some hold that this familiarity 'breaks the ice' and makes for a more friendly atmosphere, others regard it as downright rude and presumptuous. Each of us must decide for himself in the long run; but it is probably safer to keep familiarity to a minimum, not so much because it may be resented, as because it is apt to sound ludicrous. We all know the kind of thing that one hears from the more rarefied section of the BBC:

'I don't know what Sydney thinks of this point; what *do* you think, Sydney?'

'Well, Arnold, since you ask me, I think it *significant*.'

'Oh come, Sydney, that's laying it rather thickly; symbolic, I agree, but significant!'

'No, Arnold, I stand by what I said. Kruckenbacker first made this point in Vienna, you know; and you won't deny, Arnold, that Kruckenbacker covered the ground pretty thoroughly.'

'I grant that, Sydney, in fact . . .'

You see the effect? It sounds precious and affected. We could do with a return to the more formal atmosphere of earlier times in many ways, in order to restore to speech something of the dignity that it should have in public. How far we go is a matter for discretion.

THE ANATOMY OF A SPEECH

When we are browsing through novels in the public library we glance first at the title, then, if this attracts us, we open a book and read a few lines of the beginning. If these lines bore us, we return the book to the shelf at once. If you watch people in a library you will see that this is so. The listener's approach to a speech is not quite the same. People usually have to listen, whatever the beginning is like: but there is a great deal of difference between a listening which stops just short of fingers in the ears, and a listening which is eager and willing. It is with this difference that we are concerned. We want people to enjoy listening to us, not to endure it. To ensure this we must start well.

First and last impressions are important. We are apt to make up our minds about people on a first impression, though we may change our opinion later, and we carry away with us, and remember for some time, our last impression of them. The beginning of a speech, then, requires special consideration, for it sets the tone for what is to follow. It is difficult to cancel the bad impression made by a poor start to a speech and many speakers never manage to do so. The aim of the beginning is to make the audience feel that what is to follow is going to be good, going to be memorable. It is, if you like, the attractive cover which lures one into buying the contents.

The last thing the speaker should do is to begin by undermining the confidence of the audience in his ability to address them. One would have thought this so obvious that no one in his senses would do so, yet time and again we hear speakers apologizing for their very existence. What should we think of a surgeon who confessed that he was not really sure where the trouble lay but thought he could probably fish something out anyhow?

Let us look for a moment at some of these opening remarks:

(a) Ladies and gentlemen, I know you don't want to hear from me . . .

(b) You know, this kind of thing is not in my line at all . . .

(c) I'm afraid I'm not much of a speaker . . .

(d) When I was asked to speak tonight I told them I was no orator . . .

We do not need to list any more of these inane remarks. If a speaker *is* no good the audience will very quickly find that out for themselves; why should he save them the trouble?

The opening of a speech should, of course, do more than merely lull the audience into a state of false security. It should, if possible, arouse immediate interest and, if only for this reason, it should get off to a crisp, economical start and lose its effectiveness by being wrapped in verbal wadding.

Some speakers *begin* by thanking the audience for listening to them. This, though courteous and right, is out of place at the beginning of a speech. It is not even logical for they have not earned the right to be thanked until they have heard the speaker through to the end and then, goodness knows, in the case of *some* speakers they deserve all the gratitude they get.

Let us examine two possible openings for a speech opposing capital punishment, a subject much in the news lately.

Opening No 1

Ladies and gentlemen, the retention of hanging in this country is a relic of barbarism; it is no more than the old savage law of an eye for an eye and a tooth for a tooth: it appeals only to the sadist and it has no relationship with justice or humanity, but only with revenge.

Opening No 2

Ladies and gentlemen, *every year, in this country, some two hundred and fifty murderers apply for a licence to practise their trade!*

These are the psychopaths who apply to the Home Secretary for appointment as official Hangman. They are murderers, because to desire a man's death in your heart is equivalent to killing him yourself!

You will probably agree that the second opening would catch the attention of everyone at once because it is unexpected.

This is what is meant by the statement that the opening has to be different; it has to *arrest* attention, not beg for it.

PRESSING HOME THE ADVANTAGE

Just as a good boxer follows up an opening in his opponent's defence, so a good speaker follows up the initial advantage he has gained with a powerful opening. It is no good beginning well and then relapsing into generalities. You must press home your advantage.

Every speech is a series of climaxes leading, as in a stage drama, to a grand climax or end. And unity is a necessary ingredient of speech and play alike. No dramatist could afford to have one or more scenes in his play different from the rest, that is, seeming not to belong to the same play, but to have been put in by mistake from some other source.

> *Each 'point' or climax should have a clear rela-*
> *tionship with its fellow; and one should follow*
> *the other with a sense of inevitability to the final,*
> *Grand Climax.*

ACHIEVING UNITY

Before you make a speech you will, of course, plan it carefully. The best way to do this is to sit back and think round the subject in a general way first. Ideas will come at you from all sides. Don't worry about sorting them out; just let them rattle around for a while. Then, when they have settled themselves to some extent, get a piece of paper and a pencil, and write down, in précis form, the dominant ideas only. Don't bother with trivialities. Jot them all down with a couple of blank lines between each, to avoid confusion.

This is the moment to plan the beginning, along the lines already indicated. When this has been done, and you are satisfied that it is as compelling as possible, you cast about among the remaining points for the one which seems to follow most naturally from the opening, and you add the points one by one as they seem to fit best. Now you come to the second most difficult task, the ending; and this will have to be considered separately.

THE END

The ending of a speech is called the peroration. It is both an ending and a summing-up. Merely to say, 'Thank you for

57

listening; that is all I have to say,' would not do at all. The ending, like the beginning, must be *memorable*. It must be the last blow of the hammer on the nail you have been banging in throughout the speech. When you have said it, the audience should feel the *force* of it. Do please plan this with especial care. It is heartbreaking to hear a man make a good speech and then spoil it with a weak and ineffectual ending. Let us return to the speech against capital punishment. The speaker, you will recall, began on a strong note with talk of executioners as murderers. The following ending would seem to match this in mood and, at the same time, to sum up the general trend of the speech:

Those who hunt the fox sometimes point, by way of excuse, to the number of foxes which get away. Those who hunt with the rope often point out the number of monsters who deserve to die. I will only reply to that by saying that, so long as there is the possibility of there being one innocent who could *not* get away, I WILL NOT HAVE HIS BLOOD ON MY HANDS.

A speech should not aim to keep the audience on the heights of tension all the time. There must be light and shade. Shakespeare understood well how to lighten the atmosphere before a particularly dramatic scene, so as to heighten the drama by contrast; or to follow a strongly dramatic scene with a piece of comedy so that the audience should have a chance to relax before being caught up on the next wave of passion. This is well illustrated in *Hamlet,* where the funeral of the drowned Ophelia is preceded by the clowning gravediggers; and in *Macbeth,* where a drunken porter lightens the atmosphere after the terrible murder of Duncan and before the scene in which the murder is discovered.

Always try to keep your audience wondering to some extent what is coming next; and aim to leave them at the end sorry you did not speak longer. If your speech is obvious and they can see all the points coming a mile off, they will soon lose interest. A little mild mystery is a great help.

AVOIDING UNNECESSARY REPETITION

Repetition may sometimes be used deliberately for the sake of emphasis: but it must be done with great care. A word or phrase may be repeated again and again with cumulative effect, but a whole idea should not be repeated, except, perhaps (differently expressed), in the peroration as a summing-up.

It is easy to repeat oneself in a vague and pointless way without being aware of it. This spoils many speeches because the audience tires of hearing the 'same old merry-go-round'! This kind of repetition holds up the dramatic progress of the speech and leads the audience to suppose you a man of few ideas. It is wise, when you have rough-hewn your speech, to go through it looking for needless repetitions, and cut these out ruthlessly.

Sometimes it is difficult to see things if we are too close to them. For this reason it is a good idea to leave your planned speech for a day or two before revising and checking it. We all tend to feel that what we have just written, if not actually a work of genius, is a near-relation! Returning to it after a day or two, when the flush of creation has died down, we see it with a clearer eye. This is pruning time, when 'dead wood' falls easiest to the 'axe'.

If this advice were followed by all speakers we should be spared some of the more fanciful flights of oratory of the kind that goes like this:

> Our critics may think they have disheartened us, that we shall not defend the principles for which we have fought so long; but, my friends, they will find themselves hoist with their own petard; we have smelt a rat and we will clip his wings before we are much older. Let us be of a stout heart; let us march shoulder to shoulder, bearing on our broad backs the burden of our responsibility – a responsibility gladly assumed, my friends – and let us not set down our honourable load until we have reached that

goal for which we long; and the trumpets have sounded for us on the other side.

This kind of hotch-potch shows an untidy mind and a complete inability to make words work for their living. It is an exaggeration, of course; but speeches little better have been inflicted on numerous audiences at election time from representatives of all parties.

SINCERITY

There is a theory that sincerity excuses all faults. I hope no reader will be gulled by this. If it were so many of the world's feeblest speakers would be among the most successful. Many devout and sincere preachers speak so badly that they constantly cancel out the advantage of their undoubted sincerity. Sincerity is a necessary ingredient; but it is not the *only* necessary one. All ideas have to be 'sold'; even religion. Edith Cavell said: 'Patriotism is not enough.' Neither, unfortunately, is sincerity.

ACCURACY

Whenever a speech includes the quoting of facts and figures, you should ensure that they are accurate. The speaker – particularly the political speaker – has a moral right to persuade his hearers by all fair means, but this does not include the distortion of facts. It is equally distortion to deceive by omission. If you explain the answer to an equation by quoting the figures from one side only, you are clearly not being honest. An audience has a right to expect honesty from a speaker.

Sometimes figures are wrongly quoted by accident. Accidents, of course, are inevitable sometime: but careful checking before final delivery should eliminate them. You cannot be too careful about details of this kind. Apart from the deception – intentional or not – of the audience, you must bear in mind that if you are proved wrong on one set of figures, *all* your future declarations will be suspect.

Most ordinary people like ourselves – in the non-expert sense, that is – are apt to be 'dazzled into acceptance' by facts reeled out with great confidence. Unscrupulous speakers know this very well; and often score a decisive debating point by thundering: 'My friend, are you aware that between September 1977 and April 1981 no less than one hundred and fourteen *thousand* tons of bauxite were exported to Herrovia?', or something equally impressive.

These figures may, like the dates quoted, be entirely inaccurate, but we cannot prove it off-hand; and are reduced to uneasy acceptance, which gives a distinct advantage to our statistical friend.

Nothing gives more confidence than the certainty that you know your facts beyond doubt. To ensure this it is worth a few extra minutes in checking from reliable sources.

DANGER OF SARCASM

We fear the man with the acid tongue; *but we do not like him*. Sarcasm is a dangerous weapon. It *can* be effective; Mark Antony uses it effectively to rouse the Roman mob in his funeral oration for Caesar; and as a rabble-rousing weapon, a means of stirring up hatred and thoughts of revenge, it is ideal. For the ordinary speaker it is not wise. It has a habit of coming back on the speaker sooner or later.

CHOICE OF WORDS

Speakers sometimes choose their vocabulary badly, using either words which, by too-frequent usage, are tired and stale, or which sound stodgy and pompous because they are unnecessarily long. In both respects political speakers are the worst offenders, though there are some splendid exceptions.

One cannot dogmatize about vocabulary; like dress it is a matter of taste. The best one can do is to advise the speaker to choose his words on this basis – (a) Are they absolutely relevant to the meaning they are intended to express? (b) Are they the most vital and interesting words that will fulfil this condition? (c) Are they suited to the educational background of the listener?

A brilliant exception to the generalization that political speakers often choose words badly is Sir Winston Churchill. A few quotations from his speeches and writings will illustrate the importance of good choice more than any words of mine can do.

CHURCHILL ON –

Trotsky: He sits disconsolate – a skin of malice stranded for a time on the shores of the Black Sea and now washed up in the Gulf of Mexico.

Bernard Shaw: This bright, nimble, fierce, and comprehending being – Jack Frost dancing bespangled in the sunshine.

Lord Charles Beresford: He can best be described as one of those orators who, before they get up, do not know what they are going to say; when they are speaking do not know what they are saying; and when they have sat down, do not know what they have said.

The Baldwin–Chamberlain Governments: They are decided only to be undecided, resolved to be irresolute, adamant for drift, solid for fluidity, all-powerful for impotence.

The late Lord Birkenhead: Some men when they die, after busy, toilsome, successful lives, leave a great stock of scrip and securities, of acres or factories, or the goodwill of great undertakings. F.E. banked his treasure in the hearts of his friends, and they will cherish his memory till their time is come.

The speaker who cares about vocabulary will read as widely as possible and will listen as often as he can to the words of great orators and of great playwrights as expressed by actors. He will do more, though, than listen passively; he will note and recall and make use of these colourful words and phrases

62

as the occasion arises. We possess a language of incredible richness, variety, and tonal beauty and it is one of the greatest tragedies of our time that an appreciation of spoken English is now almost a rarity. Our forebears knew the value of their heritage and cherished words, using them with taste and discrimination.

A copy of *Roget's Thesaurus of English Words and Phrases,* a good dictionary, and a retentive memory will enormously increase the public speaker's range and effectiveness. *Fowler's Modern English Usage* and any – or preferably all – of the excellent Word books of Ivor Brown will also be of great value. To these must, of course, be added The Bible and a complete Shakespeare, both of which are storehouses of infinite variety and beauty in words. The speaker who is given to over-elaboration would do well to study the direct simplicity of the Authorized Version and see for himself how seventeenth-century writers made few words do much and simple words sing in the ear.

OVER- AND UNDER-STATEMENT

Over-statement should not be confused with inaccuracy. It seldom springs from careless checking or from an intention to deceive; but from uncontrolled enthusiasm.

There is a childish quality about over-statement. It smacks of the small boy's exaggeration: 'There are *hundreds* of cats in the garden; well, perhaps not hundreds, a dozen or so: well, there's our cat and the cat next door anyway!'

The danger of habitual over-statement is that, once it becomes established, your audience 'reaches for the salt' at once. 'There he goes,' they say, 'larger than life, as usual.' Not believing you becomes a habit; and they may well discount too much, even when you have sincerity and, for once, accuracy on your side.

Under-statement is regarded by foreigners – particularly from the USA – as proof of the appalling hypocrisy of the English. In fairness it should be said that it springs, more often than not, from a genuine desire not to boast or to take more than the fair share of credit: but, if overdone, it does sound immature. After all, why say 'Not bad,' when any fool can see that it is excellent?

MORE ABOUT HUMOUR

Humour has already been discussed in relation to impromptu speaking, and the same underlying principle applies here; but in a prepared speech the humour is a more deliberate matter. It has been – or *should* be – thoroughly planned. This is not always realized. 'Wonderful the way wit just flows out of that chap,' you hear people say. They do not realize that the comedian, whether on the stage or wireless, has rehearsed every one of those jokes until he has got his timing so exact that they give the *appearance* of spontaneity.

When you are delivering a prepared speech everything in it must be prepared, including the jokes, if any.

HUMOUR SHOULD ARISE NATURALLY FROM THE SUBJECT MATTER

It is wrong to view a speech as a sort of 'duff' into which a number of jokes are thrust, like currants, at random. This means that the jokes are 'out of character'. They bear no relation to the subject-matter, but are clearly just space-fillers.

A man speaking at the dinner of a golf-club, for example, is not bound to tell a funny story concerning golf, but if he tells one instead about a diver and a mermaid, it should be seen to have some relation to the theme of his discourse.

And no joke should ever be 'signalled'. We don't want to know it is coming: we want it to take us delightfully by surprise.

It would seem unnecessary to mention that whatever the humour chosen it should be appropriate to the occasion and type of audience; yet speakers offend in this way time and time again. A joke which would be highly successful at a Rugby Club Dinner might, for example, be greeted with chill disapproval at a Harvest Festival Supper!

The question of jokes in dialect is dealt with under 'Speaking at Banquets and Dinners'.

SPECIALIZED HUMOUR

. . . and the joke of it was that what the chap really had was a presystolic murmur at the apex!

This is, no doubt, a screamingly funny story when you are a doctor, nurse, or medical student; but when you are not it might as well be told in Aramaic. Humour of this kind, dependent upon knowledge of a technical vocabulary, is only effective in limited circles and it should never be used outside of them. Mechanically-minded people are perhaps the worst offenders, assuming their knowledge to be shared sufficiently for almost anyone to understand the point of the joke. Do aim to amuse *everyone*.

GETTING THE STORY RIGHT

It is most embarrassing when a speaker launches a funny story without previous preparation and becomes hopelessly involved half way because some vital point was missed. Do ensure you know the joke thoroughly, or don't begin it.

ANECDOTAL HUMOUR

Humour is one of the most valuable ingredients of spontaneous speaking and yet it is one of the most dangerous. To be able to tell a lively and amusing tale is a great advantage. Unfortunately, the joke often 'falls flat' and we are left feeling like one who has stepped on a step that wasn't there! Why is this?

It is mostly because we have mistaken the road which leads to the laugh; instead of taking the short-cut we have rambled discursively by tedious side-roads until we have lost our sparkle. What are the ingredients of a successful joke?

ECONOMY plus INCONGRUITY

Let us consider this for a moment. The first ingredient is easy to understand. A joke wrapped up in too much padding is lost in its folds. We don't want to wait long for a laugh; we want it with the minimum of introduction.

But what about incongruity? Put it this way – a clown falling into a bucket of dirty water is funny but not incongruous, because clowns are expected to do things like that. An elegantly-dressed, pompous Alderman, however, doing the same thing is hilariously funny, because we do not expect him to do anything of the kind, and we are charmed by the sudden loss of dignity. The balloon is pricked and we laugh at the explosion.

One of the most painful experiences in the world of public speaking is to have to sit through a speech by The-Life-And-Soul-Of-The-Party. We have all met him. He likes funny stories, but he cannot tell them. He usually begins with some fatuous remark as: 'Stop me if you've heard this one,' *or* 'This'll *kill* you!' and is happily unaware of the hope surging through his hearers that it will kill him instead. After what seems a lifetime the joke is finally born amid the loud guffaws of its 'parent' and is found to be a puny little monstrosity that should never have seen the light of day. We have to endure these fellows; like the Tax Inspector, they are always with us. At least we can use them as an awful warning!

If you look at a copy of *Punch* dating back to the early twenties, you will see that each cartoon had several lines of writing underneath 'explaining' the joke. This, today, is intolerably tedious, and no magazine would print such a cartoon.

Humour must speak for itself in the least number
of words.

The L-A-S-O-T-P, you see, 'signals' the climax long before he reaches it. You should never do this. The 'point' or climax of the story should catch the listener unawares and *tear* laughter from him involuntarily, not squeeze it out as an exercise in polite toleration!

As an exercise it is helpful to think of a story that has really amused you. Write it out exactly as it comes into your head. Now go through the story and reduce each sentence to the fewest number of words in which it can retain its meaning; pare it ruthlessly to almost telegraphic brevity. Now read the revised story and you will find that it is much more amusing because the 'dead wood' has been cut out. All humour – except the 'shaggy-dog' story, which has a special technique – should be pruned like this.

An example of humour in the guise of a fable with a 'moral' is 'The Unicorn In The Garden' from *Fables For Our Time* by the American humorist, James Thurber. It is contained in the book *Thurber Carnival*, published in England by Hamish Hamilton. Other recommended fables also to be found in *Thurber Carnival* are 'The Seal Who Became Famous', 'The Bear Who Let It Alone', and 'The Moth And The Star'. I once heard a speaker at a Brewers' Society Dinner recite 'The Bear Who Let It Alone' and convulse his audience.

THE USE OF QUOTATIONS

It is not wise to use quotations too often. If you do you may become a 'quotation-bore', a pedlar of other people's thoughts without an original thought of your own. But used moderately quotation can be effective. If the purpose of your quotation is to introduce a subject about which you have some original thoughts, or to illustrate a point you have just made, its use is justified; but it should never be used to display learning.

A quotation MUST be correct. A public speaker who renders Pope's line: 'A little learning is a dangerous thing' as 'a little *knowledge* is a dangerous thing' and then attributes it to Shakespeare is asking for trouble. If you are not sure of a quotation, do look it up, or leave it alone.

There are several good books of quotations available though most are expensive. A cheaper book which readers may care to consider is *The Pocket Book of Quotations* by Pocket Books Inc., of New York, edited by Henry Davidoff, and obtainable in England from most booksellers for about five shillings.

Exercises

Can you find apt quotations to illustrate:

(a) An honest man.   (c) A cynic.   (e) Flattery.
(b) A gentleman.   (d) Cruelty.   (f) Imagination.

Can you identify the following quotations?

(a) We would rather die on our feet than live on our knees.

(b) Men have died from time to time and worms have eaten them, but not for love.

NO AFTER-THOUGHTS!

A man who gets in the last word, slams triumphantly out of the door, and then has to return to ask his wife if she's seen his pipe anywhere, is apt to look foolish.

A public-speaker, having reached the last word, must resist all temptation to add something he has just thought of. To do this is to make an anti-climax. If you have prepared your peroration, don't spoil it; let the afterthought remain unborn. The part cannot be greater than the whole.

THE USE OF NOTES

If a man stands up and reads solidly from a speech written out verbatim, *he is not making a speech at all*; he is giving a reading.

Notes are reminders and no more. I once saw an earnest 'reader' at work. He was nose-down reading furiously when he suddenly realized that a page was missing. He stopped short with a half-stunned expression and scrabbled desperately among the great sheaf of paper in his hand. The missing page was nowhere to be found. The atmosphere became laden with embarrassment – his and that of his audience. Suddenly one of the platform party found the missing sheet under his chair. The speaker, now thoroughly demoralized, gabbled on demonstrably praying for the end. A single-sheet summary of a thoroughly prepared speech would have made this situation impossible.

We have already discussed the structure of a speech and have seen that it proceeds to the peroration by a series of climaxes or 'points'. Each of these points can be summarized in a few words. For a short speech one postcard will probably be large enough to contain these sentence-summaries, two or three postcards for a long speech.

If you write these simple sentences in clear, black capitals across your card, it can then either be held easily in the hand for occasional consultation, or, if you are speaking at a dinner, it can be propped up on the table before you, so that a downward glance will keep you 'on the track'.

Sheets of closely-written script are neither necessary nor useful. You don't need them – you only think you do; and even if you did, you could not follow such a mass of small script without holding it perpetually under your nose.

Never make your notes a millstone round your neck!

It may help if we study a speech – that of Queen Elizabeth I to the troops at Tilbury before the Armada in 1588. It is a fine, flamboyant piece of oratory and deserves to be studied for itself.

Queen Elizabeth I at Tilbury

My loving people, we have been persuaded by some that are careful of our safety to take heed how we commit ourselves to armed multitudes for fear of treachery.

But I assure you, I do not desire to live to distrust my faithful and loving people. Let tyrants fear. I have always so behaved myself that, under God, I have placed my chiefest strength and safeguard in the loyal hearts and goodwill of my subjects, and therefore I am come among you, as you see at this time, not for my recreation and disport, but being resolved in the midst and heat of the battle to live or die among you all, to lay down for my God and for my kingdom and for my people, my honour and my blood, even in the dust.

I know I have the body of a weak feeble woman; but I have the heart and stomach of a king, and a king of England, too, and think foul scorn that Parma or Spain, or any Prince of Europe should *dare* to invade the borders of my realm; for which, rather than any dishonour shall grow by me, *I myself* will take up arms, *I myself* will be your general, judge, and rewarder of every one of your virtues in the field.

I know already for your forwardness you have deserved rewards and crowns, *and we do assure you,* in the word of a Prince, *they shall be duly paid you.*

Elizabeth I was more than a great queen; she was a great psychologist. It was a man's world in the sixteenth century and she knew it. None could be more feminine than she when it paid her, or could curse more roundly when crossed. Note the subtle flattery of the beginning: 'I trust you even though my advisers don't.' (How Burghley must have smiled inwardly at this.) Then see how she defers prettily to the superior sex with her talk of having the body of a 'weak feeble woman'; and follows it at once with an oblique reminder that she was Henry VIII's daughter, Bluff Hal's Gal, and not to be trifled with.

See the added strength of the repetition 'I *myself*'. I, the Queen, will share your dangers with you. One can almost hear across the years the bellow of masculine approval. ('She's a rare plucked 'un'; or the Tudor equivalent.)

Then the splendid bay of defiance at the hated Spaniards, and the bellow must have changed to a dangerous growl.

Finally, the touch of shrewd calculation that was all of Elizabeth herself – the promise of pay and plunder at a time when there was no regular payment and plunder was in the lap of the gods. For a golden moment they must almost have believed her!

Now, to illustrate the advice given about summarization, let us make skeleton notes on this speech as Elizabeth might have done if so autocratic and intelligent a woman had needed even that. It will be good practice for us.

The Speech As Elizabeth Might Have Summarized It

Not afraid of treachery. Trust my people.
Will share dangers. If need be, die with you.
Only a weak woman but of a stout heart.
No European Prince shall invade my realm.
I will be your judge and general.
You deserve rewards. I will pay you well.

Exercises

Prepare in full, scripts for three-minute speeches on the following subjects; and then summarize the paragraph headings as suggested above:

1. Do We Learn From History?
2. Professionalism Has Ruined Sport.
3. The Advantages of Television.
4. How To Avoid Wars.
5. The Case For Free Trade.
6. Education For Leisure.

TWO ORATORICAL DEVICES

(a) *The Use of Parenthesis.*
(b) *Repetition for Effect.*

A parenthesis is a word, clause, or sentence inserted into a passage to which it is not grammatically essential. It is usually separated by brackets. Its use is not generally recommended because it makes the passage 'heavy' and slows up the action of the speech: but we should examine it all the same, because it *can* be used effectively on the rare occasions when the speaker wishes his words to *cut*. It conveys a contemptuous sarcasm which, unwise in the ordinary way, is necessary when something evil is to be attacked without mercy. The parenthetical remarks are spoken on a lower tone to distinguish them from the rest of the sentence or passage.

The venomous use of parenthesis is shown clearly by the following extract from a speech of William Gladstone on the Reform Bill of 1866. We must make allowances for the redundant and prosy style which was then fashionable. It is the effect of the bracketed remarks that we are concerned with.

Mr Gladstone, in a previous speech, had used the phrase: 'we know with whom we have to deal'; and the innuendo conveyed by this had brought upon him an angry rebuke from the Opposition in general and Mr Spencer Walpole in particular.

The venom lies, you will notice, not in the bracketed remarks themselves, but in the 'highlights' which follow them. The parentheses are the shadows increasing the brilliance of the succeeding phrase.

Does my right honourable friend (the Member for Calne) recollect how, in one of his plays, that Prince of comedians, Aristophanes, conveys (through the medium of some character or other) a rebuke to some prevailing tendency or sentiment of the time – (I cannot recollect now what it was – too many are the years that have slipped away since I read it, but) the character (addressing the audience) says: 'But now, my good Athenians, pray recollect I am only speaking of certain *depraved and crooked little men*'?

And if I may be permitted to make a metaphorical application of these epithets (confining myself most strictly to the metaphorical use, speaking only in a political sense, and with exclusive reference to the question of reform), I would say it was not of the House of Commons, but of '*certain depraved and crooked little men*' that I use these words, and I frankly now (in candour) own that my right honourable friend is (according to my judgment and intention) *foremost among them*; ... I think, therefore, that I am justified in using these words, significant as I admit them to be, *that we know with whom we have to deal.*

Using modern terminology we could be abusive in fewer words than Gladstone; but I doubt if we could convey better the polite venom of his '*certain depraved and crooked little men*' in our own setting.

The effect of deliberate repetition is shown in the noble speech made by Abraham Lincoln – best known as The Gettysburg Oration – in November, 1863. The whole speech has a sense of dignity and quiet resolution that places it among the finest oratory in the world.

The Gettysburg Oration

Fourscore and seven years ago our fathers brought forth upon this continent a new nation, conceived in liberty, and dedicated to the proposition that all men are created equal.

Now we are engaged in a great civil war, testing whether that nation, or any nation so conceived and so dedicated, can long endure. We have come to dedicate a portion of that field as a final resting place of those who here gave their lives that that nation might live.

It is altogether fitting and proper that we should do this. But in a larger sense *we cannot dedicate, we cannot consecrate, we cannot hallow* this ground. The brave men, living and dead, who struggled here have consecrated it far above our power to add or detract.

The world will little note, nor long remember, what we say here, but it can never forget what they did here. It is for us, the living, *rather to be dedicated here* to the unfinished work they have thus far so nobly advanced. It is *rather for us to be here dedicated* to the great task remaining before us, that from these honoured dead we take increased devotion to the cause for which they here gave the last full measure of devotion; that we here highly resolve that the dead shall not have died in vain, that the nation shall, under God, have a new birth of freedom, and that the government *of the people, by the people,* and *for the people,* shall not perish from the earth.

This speech is well worth learning by heart, not only because it is an exercise in quiet sincerity, but because of its beauty of phrase.

STUDYING FROM DRAMA

If I advise you to study speeches from stage dramas you may reply: 'I don't want to be an actor or actress; it is public speaking I am interested in.' This is quite reasonable, and yet you will be missing the most valuable source of practice if you don't widen your field of study. Read through a copy of Hansard and you will agree that most of the speeches in it are incredibly dull; they are colourless and often long-winded. These speeches will not help you. They are not what you want to produce yourself. This is not to say you are going to 'tear a passion to tatters' every time you speak in public. It only means that you should be capable of doing so eloquently when the necessity arises. Meantime, you aim to colour your speech enough to avoid melodrama but enough also to distinguish your speech from a drab, grey background.

Now here is a speech of St Joan's from Bernard Shaw's play of that name, in which she faces her Inquisitors, angry and defiant. It has lovely moments of tenderness showing through.

JOAN: Yes: they told me you were *fools,* and that I was not to listen to your fine words nor trust to your charity. You promised me my life; but you lied.

(a)   You think that life is nothing but not being stone dead. It is not the bread and water I fear: I can live on bread: when have I asked for more? It is no hardship to drink water if the water be clean. Bread has no sorrow for me, and water no affliction.

(b)
But to shut me from the light of the sky and the sight of the fields and flowers; to chain my feet so that I can never again ride with the soldiers nor climb the hills; to make me breathe foul damp darkness, and keep me from everything that brings me back to the love of God when your wickedness and foolishness tempt me to hate Him: all this is worse than the furnace in the Bible that was heated seven times.

(c) 1.
I could do without my war-horse; I could drag about in a skirt: I could let the banners and the trumpets and the knights and soldiers pass me and leave me behind as they leave the other women, if

(c) 2.
only I could still hear the wind in the trees, the larks in the sunshine, the young lambs crying through the healthy frost, and the blessed, blessed church bells that send my angel voices floating to me on the wind.

(d)
But without these things I cannot live: and by your wanting to take them away from me, or from any human creature, I know that your counsel is of the *Devil*, and that mine is of *God*. . . . His ways are not your ways. He wills that I go through the

(e)
fire to his bosom; for I am his child, and you are not fit that I should live among you. That is my last word to you.

When you read this speech remember that Joan is a dual-personality: in one part a tough, peasant girl, contemptuous of femininity and well able for the daily rough-and-tumble of a foot soldier; and in the other part of her a mystic and dreamer, desiring a martyrdom that will bring her to God. For convenience in analysis the speech has been divided into emotional groups and each group has a distinguishing letter.

(a)   The beginning is strong. The first sentence calls forth an angry reaction from the Inquisitors. Joan is furious because they have lied to her. Then comes the note of contempt on the line 'You think that life is nothing but not being stone dead.'

(b)   Joan's voice reflects nausea more than fear. She speaks with the loathing of someone describing a repulsive sight.

(c) 1.   Again the note of contempt. This is strongest on the line 'I could drag about in a skirt.' (Joan has little use for women who do so.)

(c) 2.   Here a lyrical note creeps in and Joan's voice softens and she speaks more slowly. We should feel that she sees these desirable things in her mind's eye as clearly as she saw the foetid dungeon. There is an especially tender and longing note on the phrase 'blessed, blessed church bells that send my angel voices floating to me on the wind'. (The Inquisitors do not believe in Joan's angel voices.)

(d)   Mounting passion drives her voice up until it rings out on the phrase 'and that mine is of God'.

(e)   There is here a complete change. Joan the soldier has become Joan the martyr, the dedicated soul. The voice is quiet, unemotional, almost a little-girl voice that has withdrawn from this world and already sees its salvation in the next. There is dignity and reproof rather than the former contempt on the line '. . . and you are not fit that I should live among you. That is my last word to you'. No dramatic rendering here in the robustious sense. Quiet and very firm and resigned. With this line Joan cuts her last tie with life and is content to do so.

MISCELLANEOUS EXERCISES

1. Prepare skeleton notes for three-minute speeches on:

   (*a*) Travel brochures.   (*b*) Faith.   (*c*) Freedom.

2. Write down the most compelling OPENING paragraphs for speeches on:

   (*a*) The duties of a citizen.
   (*b*) Love as a total delusion.
   (*c*) Modern art.
   (*d*) The futility of war.

3. Write down and *reduce to its bare essentials* your favourite funny story.

4. Make a list of all the political clichés you can think of.

5. Prepare full notes for a five-minute speech on one of the following subjects, and then summarize the notes on a plain postcard:

   (*a*) My favourite hobby. (*b*) A book that has moved me.
   (*c*) My favourite fictional character.

6. Prepare a speech of not less than three minutes duration for an audience of ten-year-old boys and girls, on 'Hobbies For the Winter Months'.

7. Can you find apt quotations for:

   (*a*) An impulsive person.
   (*b*) A foolish ruler.
   (*c*) A fallen dictator.
   (*d*) The advantages of imagination.

8. Write down some unhackneyed phrases you might use to describe:

   (*a*) An atomic power station. (*b*) A sheep round-up.
   (*c*) A naval mock-battle. (*d*) A revivalist meeting.

9. Prepare a full-length speech for or against the idea of a future military alliance with Germany.

10. Prepare a speech of welcome – *not* to exceed three minutes – for:

(*a*) A famous athlete. (*b*) An American oil 'king'. (*c*) A notorious writer of lurid thrillers. (*d*) A famous comedy couple of stage or screen. (*e*) A great actor.

AFTER-DINNER SPEAKING

The after-dinner speech must be considered in a different way to any other kind of speech because it is part of a social entertainment and is accompanied by eating and drinking. The accent is on pleasure.

It is unfortunate that many otherwise delightful social occasions are spoiled by the speech-making. Just as one is mellowing under the influence of good food and drink, the companionship of one's fellows and the feeling of well-being that wearing one's best clothes usually evokes, one is compelled to listen politely to a series of speeches many of which are badly-prepared and most of which are too long.

The after-dinner speech should *never* be long, however good the speaker. It should be light and witty and as digestible as the food.

George Jessel, the famous American toastmaster, is said to have invented the saying: 'If you don't strike oil in five minutes STOP BORING.' One can hardly think of better advice.

The speaker will have less cause for anxiety at the prospect of speaking after dinner if he thinks less of what he can offer and more about what he, in the listener's place, would expect. If he is honest with himself he will certainly conclude that what he wants primarily is brevity and secondarily entertainment. With this in mind he can begin to think about composing the speech that will fulfil both these conditions.

First, he should try to bear in mind that his audience – unless they are singularly different from the average – do not expect him to display a Churchillian brilliance in his speaking, so he can save himself the trouble of trying to be clever; it seldom succeeds.

Next, he must prepare with great care an interesting beginning, bearing in mind the general 'theme' of his speech and the type of audience he is to address. Then, before he starts to work on the main body of his speech he will do well to plan just where he will end it and in what way. More speeches are ruined by an unplanned ending than by almost any other fault. Because a clear and decisive ending has not been planned the speaker 'wiffles' on vaguely, casting around desperately in his mind for a point at which to cease, and in this state of mental confusion repeats himself over and over again until he panics into an ending that lacks punch or even relevance.

As for what goes in the middle, like a sandwich-filling, that depends upon so many considerations that it is impossible to do more than offer general advice. One cannot successfully write another man's after-dinner speech for him. It is too personal a thing, too dependent upon the speaker's personality, the type of audience and their mood at the moment of speaking and upon the speaker's ability to seize lightly and easily upon something that has already been said and to make capital out of it.

The reader may find that, in his own case, wittiness does not come easily, if at all. In this case he will be well advised to keep his speech sincere and 'straight' but without stodginess and leave wit to some other speaker. In the end sincerity never loses. We can forgive a lack of wit; but we will not forgive insincerity or verbosity.

Wit, when it is used, should arise in the most spontaneous and natural way. It should never be laboured or lengthy. Advantage may be taken of something said by another speaker to make a witticism out of it but this should always be in the spirit of good clean fun. In this connexion the Rev. John Watson (Ian Maclaren) lecturing in the United States said:

If I had the power to give humour to the nations I would not give them drollery, for that is impractical; I would not give them wit, for that is aristocratic, and many minds cannot grasp it; but I would be content to deal out fun, which has no intellectual element, no subtlety, belongs to old and young, educated and uneducated alike, and is the natural form of the humour of the Englishman.

One of the funniest speeches I have ever listened to was delivered, poker-faced, by a dry little clergyman who had just come to a neighbouring parish from an African mission where he had spent the greater part of his life. The occasion was a very humble one – a harvest social and supper – and the audience, for the most part, ordinary, unsophisticated people. The little man stood quietly for something under five minutes while fun simply flowed out of him. He said nothing that was brilliant or intellectual and afterwards it was difficult to recall any particularly memorable phrase he had used; but we all laughed loudly and unashamedly and felt the better for it. As an after-meal speech it was a thundering success and I envied him his triumph.

I think the secret of his success was that the fun he created was based upon genuine experience, was kindly and sympathetic, never patronizing and had at its core, a real affection for the simple African people who were concerned in it.

He told of an elderly priest whose long celibacy had made him old-maidishly fussy about trifles and who had a particular liking for buttered toast – perhaps because it was so essentially English. But the toast had to be crisp; he could not endure it soggy and the Mission cook could never seem to produce it any other way. The priest read the cook a great lecture one day on the art of making toast white-man-style, and ended up with the statement that pieces of toast should never be laid upon each other when made as this led to sogginess. They must be kept upright and separate, he said. For several weeks after this the toast came to the table as crisp as the heart of man could desire and the old priest was delighted. Wishing to express his appreciation he paid a special visit to the kitchen and found the cook making more toast while holding the pieces already made upright and separate between the toes of his left foot! I suppose that really this is not such a funny story; indeed, the sensitive may find it slightly nauseating;

but I know we all roared at it. Which only goes to prove that it is not so much *what* is said as *how* it is said that counts.

It is difficult to advise students what to say next when they have 'broken the ice' because an after-dinner speech is a kind of vocal cocktail and the ingredients and shaking are subject to last-minute alterations. What you say next depends so much on circumstances at the time, the common bond that binds the listeners (rugby-players, philatelists, brewers and their wives, etc.) and the content of any speeches which may have preceded yours. *This is where every moment you have spent practising spontaneous speech is going to pay you golden dividends.*

You should, since we have assumed previous warning, have prepared a speech on broad lines, but, for the reasons given above, you may have to alter, extend or reduce this as you go. Do not let this worry you. It will come easily. If you are relaxed, if you have prepared a speech at all, if you are enjoying the wine, savouring the food and admiring the company, your vocal 'red carpet' will roll itself out at your feet, and you will dance happily down the middle of it when your time comes.

Enjoyment is delightfully infectious

Have you ever sat in a theatre near to a man with a loud, hearty laugh. If the show is not very funny, or it doesn't seem so to you anyway, this laugh irritates you at first. But after a little while you find you are laughing heartily too, though the show is really no better than it was. You have caught the infection, you see, and you are laughing in spite of yourself. (Please do not take this as an invitation to laugh at your own jokes!) Seriously, your whole success as an after-dinner speaker is dependent upon your passing on to the audience as strongly as possible, a sense of your own untrammelled enjoyment of the occasion.

AFTER-DINNER HUMOUR

With the emphasis on enjoyment humour is a serious business, paradoxical though that may sound. In the ordinary way, an audience may show disapproval of your jokes by actually saying so, or by coughing and shuffling inattentively: but not at a Dinner. There is nothing they can do at a Dinner but suffer. Courtesy even demands that they smile and clap at the end, though their motive may be gratitude for release rather than appreciation of the joke. Bearing this in mind, you will see that the speaker who tries to pass off a few stale jokes as entertainment is taking advantage of his special immunity; and he will not be easily forgiven.

It is said that there is no such thing as a new joke; they have all been told before. This may be so; but it does not prevent an old joke having a new look. The approach can be different. Try to make after-dinner jokes short and light.

The audience has enough to do to digest the dinner; they don't want the speeches to be heavy going too! All that has been said about humour earlier applies equally here, but the emphasis should be even heavier on brevity.

A golfing story that may illustrate the point about brevity, concerns a four-ball match:

> The first player swung badly and said: 'Lord! what a slice!'
> The second followed suit and snarled: 'What a ghastly hook!'
> The third player took a tremendous swipe and roared: 'Topped the "asterisk" again!'
> The fourth man swung violently three times without touching the ball at all, smiled gently and said: *'Tough course!'*

THE DIALECT JOKE

At a Dinner given by the Irish Bowling Association an Irishman, proposing a toast to 'The Visitors', told what was an otherwise good story about an Englishman, in an excruciating imitation of Cockney speech. Replying for the visitors, an Englishman – more daring – told a story about an Englishman, an Irishman, and a Scot. His Irish and Scots dialect was, if possible, even worse than the Irishman's 'Cockney'.

Each national speech has its distinctive pronunciations. These are not difficult to learn, and this fact encourages people to imagine that learning the pronunciation is sufficient. It is not. The real subtlety of dialect lies in its *inflections*, and unless these are right the rest of the imitation will not compensate. You can say: 'Sure I didn't see the man at all' and not sound remotely like an Irishman unless you have the 'tune' right.

If you can tell a dialect story well it is a popular form of humour; but if you give a painful approximation it will fall flat. Use it only if you know the pattern and the tune are authentic. Otherwise it is best left alone.

If you are keen to 'work up' a particular kind of speech – Irish, Scots, Welsh, Lancashire, and so on, special study records are obtainable.

SOME MORE ABOUT STANCE

On other occasions a speaker should be quite at ease with his hands loosely and unselfconsciously by his side. At a Dinner, however, *one* hand lightly in the pocket is permissible, and gives just that touch of informality that the occasion warrants. *Both* hands in the pockets is always wrong; it is slovenly and can look positively rude and objectionable.

Owing to the positioning of the tables, it is sometimes difficult to appear to be talking to everyone at once; but do try to sweep each section with your eye in turn so that no one will feel ignored.

The head should be kept well up. We have all seen speakers mumble into the table-cloth. The focal path of the voice should be along a line from the mouth inclining up to a point a foot or so higher at the limit of pitch.

There should be no play with handkerchiefs, wine-glasses, or any other kind of 'prop'. Repose is necessary if you are to gain the confidence of your hearers. We are all impressed by the person who appears calm and utterly self-controlled.

It is always dangerous to live through circumstances before they happen, to experience them by anticipation. If a man hesitates outside the door of a crowded room saying to himself: 'It will be like this or that. Mr A will say so-and-so, Mrs Y will say such-and-such, Miss B will make me feel inferior, and the whole N family will snub me,' he is more than likely to be taken aback when those conditions he has anticipated do not match his actual experience, and he is left with a set of 'prepared reactions' which are now useless because they do not fit. Public speakers often live ahead of themselves like this; and are flustered by reality. As Sydney Smith said:

> '*A great deal of talent is lost to the world for want*
> *of a little courage.*'

You can seldom go wrong with public speaking if you are genuinely interested in your fellows, because in ourselves there is infinite variety. Observation of people as they are, and not as you think they ought to be, and an honest revelling in the abundance of their sins as well as their virtues – always remembering that your own are included – will give you a bottomless well of wisdom and experience from which to draw material for talking about people.

Rudyard Kipling, who savoured humanity with an immense and comprehending joy, wrote:

> *In the absence of angels, who I am sure would be*
> *horribly dull, men and women are the most fascinating*
> *things in the whole wide world.*

How does all this affect stance, you ask? It affects it *vitally*. You will stand and look as you feel. The speaker who shrinks mentally shrinks physically; he is not rejoicing in his fellows but fearing them: it is written in every sinew of his body. Think well of what you are doing and you will do it well and look well too. Head up, body relaxed, a pleasant appearance and a bright and cheerful eye. This ... can ... be ... YOU if you will it to be. Only you can decide.

TACT

A desire to be humorous sometimes leads to tactlessness, and we should be careful about this; once the words are out we cannot recall them, and a last-minute attempt to 'pick up' a dropped 'brick' makes the situation worse, not better. An example of this is a serious gaffe made at a Banquet by a Scotsman whose home was in the best salmon-fishing area of his country. There had been salmon on the menu, and in the course of his speech he referred to it by saying that where *he* came from they knew what salmon really was and would use that kind as bait! This was not intended to be rude, but it could hardly have sounded worse.

RIDING ONE'S HOBBY-HORSE

We sometimes hear one man say of another: 'Old Bill's a bit of a fanatic on rose-growing' (or whatever his interest may be); and more of us fit the description than are aware of it. Most of us can ride our hobby-horses if given some small encouragement – or even if not! We must be chary of such exercise at Dinners or other social occasions, though, because a subject that is quite enthralling to us may be boring to almost everyone else. If *your* hobby-horse was (say) calendar reform, it would be a breach of good manners to introduce it at length into a speech at the annual Dinner of the local Rugby Club, using club fixtures as a thin excuse. The members and guests are likely to be interested in the fixtures and completely indifferent to the reform of the calendar.

Before leaving the subject of Dinners, please consider a few encouraging facts:

(*a*) For the subject of your speech you have the wide world to roam in and are bounded only by the rules of good taste.

(*b*) As your purpose is to entertain you may be fantastical, lightly humorous, mock-serious, or wholly serious in an undemanding vein.

(*c*) To establish friendly relations with your fellows – even for the space of a few hours – is to live *positively*.

(*d*) To have made a creditable speech and been rightly applauded is a gain to one's self-respect and a step by which one can climb higher next time.

The clever man makes hay with the grass that grows under his rival's feet.

TALKING TO CHILDREN

Any actor will tell you that a performance given specially for children is a delightful experience – always provided, of course, that a suitable play has been selected.

The child's capacity to think imaginatively, to become completely absorbed in what he sees and hears, makes him a ready and attentive listener, uninhibited in his reactions and loudly generous in his praise.

But, no adult can so quickly withdraw his attention or retreat into another world so completely as can a child who is bored with the proceedings, for in this respect also children have no inhibitions and are not deterred by considerations of 'proper' social behaviour. When a young child is bored he does not care who knows it. He quite simply 'switches off' in his mind. For this reason anyone unaccustomed to talking to audiences of children should tread very warily indeed when doing so. I do not mean that children are an 'awkward' audience. They are most willing to enjoy themselves and to go more than half way to meet an entertainer; but he must entertain not *preach*. It is possible to get home a moral when talking to children without their being aware that you are doing so; but the pill must be well-sugared for children even more than adults dislike being 'got at' and will give a lukewarm reception to a speaker whom they suspect is doing this.

Children like illustration and are fascinated by how things work, so, if it is at all possible, talks to children should contain some visual element, either in pictorial or cinematic form. You can teach children how to deal with minor First Aid crises much more effectively if you smear one of them with a little tomato sauce, wrap him in bandages and tell him he is a casualty than you can by describing what a casualty would look like.

In no circumstances should a speaker adopt a patronizing manner to children, however young. Their youth does not preclude intelligence and many youngsters these days are extremely intelligent and have an unquenchable thirst for knowledge, so long as it is seen to be worth acquiring and has an apparent relevance to their lives.

It is wiser, however, to ask children to reserve their questions until the talk is concluded, otherwise the speaker may well find himself swamped with questions and unable to reach the conclusion he had planned.

While it is not necessary to talk to children in the language of *Chick's Own*, it *is* necessary to use a simplified vocabulary. It is easy for an adult to imagine that because he understands the meaning of a word his young listeners will understand it also. This is not always the case.

Speakers sometimes indulge in rather subtle humour when talking to young children and this is not wise, for children do not often appreciate subtle wit, preferring something of the more frankly slapstick variety. This is not a question of intelligence but of natural development. Mankind is not born subtle or sophisticated.

I remember being asked once if I approved of adults using slang expressions when talking to children and I found this hard to answer categorically. Probably a too-free use of slang is unwise but it is undeniable that many slang expressions are so much more colourful and lively than their formal counterparts that they would appeal more to a young listener. If the speaker is to use slang he should be careful to keep it up-to-date. Nothing dates so quickly as slang as anyone who was a Greyfriars fan in his youth will recall. No schoolboy now describes something as 'topping' and it is better to be an ordinary 'square' than an out-of-date one.

Children have their own code of morals; actually children are very *moral*, on the whole. They like right to conquer wrong, though not without casualties on both sides and are apt to be intolerant of compromise. When we are ten years of age our whites are very white and our blacks very black; we are not much in favour of shades in between. For this reason children love melodrama and their villains cannot be too villainous or their heroes too heroic. They are, however (and rightly, indeed), impatient of do-gooders and the wise speaker will never try to point a moral by using any Eric-or-Little-by-Little type as an illustration.

Children love action, frequent, violent, and exciting action, so if you are going to tell them a story by way of illustration or light relief, get to the point with all speed. Never perambulate. Short and meaty is the motto.

Speakers, from time to time, find themselves foxed by some particularly searching question asked by a young listener, and when this happens it is unwise to bluff. A child can be astonishingly perceptive and you will lose face far more by a bluff that is called than you will by a frank admission that you do not know, though in the latter case it is better to add the assurance that you will find out as soon as possible.

Finally, it is always a good idea to let a child express his ideas in his own way; do not put words into his mouth and do please praise him when he asks an intelligent question or expresses an original idea. A little judicious praise goes a long way. Children should be encouraged to be individuals, not educated puppets.

NOW FOR COLLEGES AND YOUTH GROUPS

This section concerns children from twelve to eighteen or so, at which latter age they are, in all but experience, men and women. We are on shifting soil here, because the years of puberty and adolescence have difficulties not experienced in the junior stages.

First of all, we have to remember that children mature much earlier today than they did twenty years or more ago. Girls of fourteen today look like women of eighteen or twenty and sometimes behave like them. They mature more rapidly than boys and acquire self-possession earlier. But these are largely physical changes. At heart most of them are still children, with a child's need of reassurance, though they might die rather than admit it.

Adolescence is a stage when we are neither children nor adults; we have the need of children for affection and security, but we have the desire of adults for independence, and are beginning to have adult sexual desires as well, which adds to the uncertainty of our position. We feel that we have a foot in either camp, and are never certain of which we are really belonging to. This makes us touchy and shy, longing for security but afraid that asking for it will brand us as childish. It is a very difficult stage of development.

All this must be borne in mind when you are talking to Colleges or groups of older children. They must be treated with *scrupulous courtesy* and absolutely no trace of condescension. All children should be treated politely and will usually reply in kind; but it is more important than ever with adolescents, because of their need to preserve their dignity. After all, it is hard for a huge six-footer with an incipient moustache to be treated like a scrubby little boy because he is still at school. He may have a lot to learn – and he usually knows it as well as you do – but it isn't kind to rub it in.

With intelligent older children it is necessary to prepare your lecture in great detail. They are accustomed to taking a good deal of fairly difficult instruction daily and working on it at home in the evenings. They are developing critical qualities, especially those destined for the university, and you must know your subject, because they will probe mercilessly if they suspect a weakness, or believe you to be bluffing on a point.

Speaking to these older children is easier from the point of view of vocabulary, of course, because they are usually well-read and discuss ideas freely among themselves. They will be hurt if you appear to be choosing your own words at too simple a level.

SUMMARY OF THE ESSENTIAL POINTS

Go straight to the point.
Plenty of action.
Minimum of descriptive detail.
Accuracy.
No condescension.
Suitable vocabulary.
Scrupulous politeness.
No bluffing.

DEBATING AND PRIVATE ARGUMENT

Debating (and private argument at its best) is distinguished from other kinds of public speech by the extent to which it appeals to reason rather than to emotion.

In an argument – and for all practical purposes we can include a debate in this term – we seek to persuade our hearers by a process of reasoned steps leading to an inescapable conclusion. Clearly, then, we must take pains to ensure that the steps by which we ascend to that conclusion are not faulty, else the conclusion will be faulty also.

One of the world's funniest sights is that of a man sitting happily on the branch of a tree, and sawing hard between the trunk and himself. 'No one would be such a fool,' you will say. Perhaps not physically; but mentally, yes – every day. Many of us defeat our own arguments while insisting that we are being thoroughly logical. 'Stands to reason, old boy,' we say, sawing away regardless!

To take a hypothetical case. Suppose we have a Communist tub-thumping in Hyde Park. In the course of a long harangue he makes the following points:

1. It is time for a new regime founded on the *equality of man*. Capitalism has done nothing for mankind only made millions for individuals. *We stand for freedom.*

2. *Only those who produce have a right to the profits of their labour.* They say we are irresponsible to strike, *but every man has a right to dispose of his own labour.*

3. *The bosses think they can fool the worker with their Welfare Schemes,* and free this-and-that; but we can see through that all right.

4. *There is no room in a Communist State for bosses or non-producers. We will share all profits equally. The state can give full employment as easily as the bosses.*

5. Blacklegs who refuse to join with their comrades in strikes *must be crushed* like the parasites they are.

6. When the Communist State is achieved *we shall be ruled by those who fought for it,* not by money-grubbing plutocrats.

7. *We will destroy the black-coated slaves* and boot-lickers who kept the bosses in power as they would have destroyed us.

What has this orator really said? Let us analyse it.

Statement – 'We stand for freedom.'

> But, in (5) he advocates crushing those who do not agree with him, in (7) promises to destroy them, and in (2) he says every man has a *right* to dispose of his own labour!

Statement – 'It is time for a new regime founded on equality.'

But, in (2) he denies equal rights to all, in (4) he says there is *no room* for bosses or non-producers, and in (6) he says the new bosses will be those who fought for freedom.

Statement – 'Capitalism has done nothing for mankind.'

But, in (3) he speaks of the bosses' 'Welfare Schemes' and in (4) he admits that the bosses have given full employment.

Statement – 'We will share all profits equally.'

But, in (2) only those who *produce* have a right to a share at all; and in (7) the black-coated workers, being ear-marked for destruction, are not intended to have a share either.

To this man an opponent is not necessary because he has defeated all his own arguments. It is clear that he thinks all men are equal but some are more equal than others!

It is easy to confound one's own arguments without being aware of it. In debating we should take pains to examine carefully all the points we intend to make, to see that none of them contradicts another in this way.

THE 'NON SEQUITUR'

This is the name given to a mistaken reasoning in which we infer a conclusion which does not rightly follow from the first statement. It is very common.

'He plays tennis; he must be athletic.'
'He owns a yacht; he must be a gentleman.'
'He reads a lot; he must be clever.'

THE 'RED HERRING'

This is the name given to an irrelevant issue which distracts attention from the proper subject of the debate. An example would be as follows:

Argument: Subject – Blood Sports

John: Blood sports are disgusting. I don't know how we can call ourselves British while we torture animals for fun.

Dick: If you are thinking of fox-hunting, foxes are vermin you know. If we didn't kill them the farmers would soon complain.

John: I know that, but it's the beastliness of it all. How would you like to be chased and torn to pieces by dogs? And that horrible business of 'blooding' children.

Dick: In its wild state a fox can expect to be chased by other animals; I don't see that it makes any difference because —

John: It's just an excuse for snobbery, for dressing up in pink coats and silly hats and drinking stirrup cups. It's childish, really.

Dick: Oh, I don't know. It's a part of the traditional background in England. I don't think we should cut our links with the past. And it's quite democratic, you know. Lots of farmers ride to hounds, and they aren't aristocrats.

John: Farmers are wealthy people these days. Ordinary people like us can't afford to follow the hunt. . . .

I am sure you will have spotted the 'red herring' by now. The argument, you see, was about the *cruelty* of blood sports, not about their *social significance*; but as soon as John mentioned snobbery they were both away after the 'red herring' at full tilt. We should try to see a straight line in all our arguments and to follow it rigorously, refusing to be turned aside by irrelevant arguments; otherwise we find we have spent our time arguing about all kinds of things which have nothing to do with the subject we intended to discuss.

RATIONALIZING

Sometimes we are so anxious to believe something that we believe it first and look for reasons in support of our belief afterwards. A woman who wants to believe that a man is in love with her uses this process of rationalization to 'prove' it. She decides he *is* in love with her, and then says 'I know he is because . . .', and she invents reasons in support of her statement. Often she is quite right, of course; but not always.

This rationalizing is harmless in most cases – a man wants to eat steak and chips and argues that it must be all right, whatever the doctor said, because . . .; a small boy wants to 'skip' his Latin homework and go fishing, so he concludes first that it would be wrong to do his homework just then and produces half a dozen arguments to prove his case. We all do it in support of harmless self-indulgences. It is when this process is applied to major matters that it becomes evil. The Nazi Party, seeking a scapegoat for German internal troubles and demoralization after the First World War, decided to blame the Jewish people, so they gave the infamous Julius Streicher – Editor of *Die Sturmer* – and later Goebbels, the order to rationalize this conclusion by any and every means, with the tragic results we have seen.

Rationalization is harmless in small ways, but we should be able to recognize the technique when we use it or encounter it.

LOGIC AND INFALLIBILITY

It is easy to be led astray by applying mathematical principles to human behaviour. Thus we lead from primary assumptions into absurdity. It is not unknown for people to arrive at conclusions as false as that below, by doing this.

Statement: Two men can carry a piano upstairs in four minutes.

Conclusion: One man could carry the piano upstairs in eight minutes.

The process of 'reasoning' used here leads us to make conclusions such as:

(*a*) John Smith never smoked or drank and he lived to be a hundred years old. *Therefore,* abstaining from smoking and drinking is the secret of living to a 'ripe old age'.

(b) The instructions say: 'A tablespoonful three times a day'. *Therefore,* if I take a tablespoon six times a day I shall get well in half the time.

AGREEMENT UPON 'TERMS OF REFERENCE'

Much bad temper is engendered by the fact that people sometimes think they are arguing about the same thing, when in fact they are not. This is because they have not agreed on their terms of reference. If James's definition on an 'honest' man is a man who would, in no circumstances, accept a bribe, and John's definition of an 'honest' man is one who *would* accept a bribe in certain circumstances but would make no secret of the fact, it is clear that these two men will never agree about the meaning of 'honest' because each defines that meaning in a different way.

We are not likely to experience this confusion about concrete objects, but when we come to abstractions, mental states, we must be sure we are arguing about the same thing as our opponent is. It is a waste of time to argue about the merits of democracy, or totalitarianism, or any other way of life, unless we both mean the same thing when we use the same word.

The American Declaration of Independence (1776) contains the following statement:

> We hold these *truths* to be self-evident: that *all men are created equal*; that they are endowed by their *Creator* with certain *inalienable rights*; that among these are *life, liberty*, and the pursuit of *happiness*.

Considered as an attempt to dignify and elevate the status of men in the eyes of their fellow-men, this is an admirable and beautifully-phrased passage; but as an explicit statement which could be generally agreed, it is quite useless. Consider the terms:

Truth: Pontius Pilate asked: 'What is truth?' and men have been arguing on the answer ever since. If, as the scientists tell us, no two people can ever see quite the same mental image as each other, how can we agree on what is true or not true?

Equality: Are all men created equal? If we believe this to be so do we all practise the way of life inferred from the statement? Did Adolf Hitler? Does Johannes Strijdom? or are some 'more equal than others'? What do *you* mean when you say 'freedom'?

Rights: What are 'rights'? If I have a 'right' to live, have I also a 'right' to die when I choose, or to take another's life by judicial execution?

Liberty: Liberty to do what? If I am not at liberty to burn down my own house when I am tired of looking at it, is 'liberty' worth having? What does it mean anyway? If we restrict the liberty of a man to do this or that within the community, do we not thus deny the existence of liberty at all?

Happiness: The film-star with five ex-husbands, alimony, wealth in jewels and possessions and universal adulation . . . is she 'happy'?

The monk in the seclusion of an enclosed order, vowed to silence and contemplation and with no possessions beyond bare necessities . . . is he happy?

You and I and millions of ordinary people with limited means, unexceptionable tastes and a fair share of anxieties . . . are we 'happy' and *can we be sure we would know for certain when we were?*

GENERALIZATION

When we generalize we accept the circumstances attendant upon one thing as applying equally to many things of the same kind. In short, we jump to a conclusion upon insufficient evidence.

Suppose I observe that, although Henry is forty years old and his wife, Joan, is only eighteen, their marriage is a happy one, should I be wise to assume from this that all marriages in which there was a similar disparity in ages would be equally happy?

If I meet a Frenchman who behaves with almost hysterical excitement over some trivial matter, should I be correct in assuming that *all* Frenchmen are of an hysterically excitable disposition?

A duck-egg has made me ill. Would it be correct to argue from this that *all* duck eggs are dangerous and you would be unwise to follow my example in eating one?

Jumping to unwarranted conclusions in this manner is commonly encountered, and it leads to such sweeping statements as

{ The Irish all love fighting and drinking.
{ The Irish are all sentimental and ultra-patriotic.
{ The English are snobbish and unfriendly.
{ The English are shameless imperialists.
{ Germans are cruel and aggressive.
{ The only good German is a dead one!

Generalizations are insidiously dangerous because they are so apt to slip past unrecognized; familiarity has made them a part of the landscape.

THE 'LEADING' QUESTION

A 'leading' question starts with an assumption which may not be true. If you ask me 'Why are women tidier then men?' I cannot answer you until it has been established that women *are* in fact tidier than men. Only then could I seek for the reason. This little 'trick' can lead one up dangerous pathways in argument and we should be on the look out for it.

SOME ADVICE ON FORMAL DEBATING

Formal debates require leading and secondary speakers for each side. Supposing you, for the moment, to be the leading speaker, what advice can be given you?

First, examine what you have to do. If we assume the subject of your Debate to be that 'This House asserts that the Middle Class has cut its own throat', and you are the principal speaker in favour of that motion, your first responsibility is to agree with your supporting speaker upon the 'line' you are going to adopt in favour of the contention.

It will be a good idea to write down in the least number of words the 'points' you intend to make. These points may first be written as they occur to you; but later you and your co-speaker should arrange them in the order of presentation. It is best not, at this stage, to divide your responsibilities.

Summary of 'Points' to be Made

1. By its very name the 'middle' class condemns itself, for, like a sandwich filling, it is under pressure from above and below!

2. The upper classes do not hesitate to protect their own interests by such means as hereditary legislation (the Lords) and the exclusiveness of certain appointments, kept for public-schoolboys and contacts made in exclusive clubs and societies. The working classes have no hesitation in preserving their interests by militant trades-unionism; but the middle class is too 'superior' to associate with the working class, and not superior enough to associate with the upper class.

3. This 'touch-me-not' attitude to those below leaves the middle class struggling along, trying to 'keep up appearances', trying to 'go one better than the Joneses' and voting for politicians who use their snobbish fears to keep them in subjection. They are always the first to suffer from increases in the cost of living because they have no collective bargaining power and are too selfish to join together to gain some.

These three main points contain enough minor and supporting points to keep a debate going happily for quite a long time. Would you be wise, having agreed upon this with your co-speaker, to leave it at that? You would not indeed.

A good general tries to imagine himself in the opposing general's place and works out thus the enemy's next probable move. The debater should do the same.

You should examine every argument that your opponent

is likely to use. He will be likely, for instance, to try to show that the class divisions in Britain are fluid and are constantly changing, so that a working-class family in one generation becomes a middle-class family in the next, and so on. You should be prepared, whenever possible, to quote facts and figures in support of your contention, and to quote what famous people have said on the subject.

An argument is always more likely to carry conviction if it is supported by evidence of this kind. Had the subject of the debate been: 'This House approves of Irish Partition', and Smith, as principal speaker, been referring to the attitude of Ulster to the Home Rule Bill of 1920, he should have been able to say with authority that when this Bill was introduced no Irish Member voted for it; but it was passed and *accepted by Ulster*.

You must know your argument thoroughly before you begin the Debate. It will be too late to 'look up' details in the middle of it.

The supporting speaker's job is not that of a mere echo; he should not repeat in different words what his leader has said: but amplify the 'line' of the leader's speech in persuasive terms, answering on the way any minor points that the opposition may have made since. He must be ready to counter opposition points on his leader's behalf.

For practice you might like to work out arguments for or against some of the following Motions:

1. That this House regards Compulsory Military Service as an ineffective measure of defence.

2. That this House believes British citizenship to be too easily awarded; and holds that it should be withdrawn when the holder has disgraced it.

3. That this House favours the adoption of Proportional Representation.

4. That this House denies the need of all for secondary grammar education and maintains that many now receiving it would be better off without it.

5. That this House views with alarm the ill effect of television upon the social habits of the community.

6. That this House demands the standardization of fines and penalties in Magistrates' Courts for minor offences.

7. That this House deplores the influence on speech and manners of Transatlantic cinema and stage shows.

8. That this House has no confidence in the present government.

9. That this House favours the outlawing of the Communist Party.

10. That this House holds present Trades Union practices to be obstructive and damaging to the national prosperity.

THE PUBLIC SPEAKER'S CHECK-CHART

The Speech from Conception to Birth

1. Decision to speak and selection of subject.
2. Choice of speaking time.
3. Free imaginative thought around subject.
4. *All* ideas jotted down at random.
5. Ideas graded in importance and a strong ending and beginning selected. The ending may be planned first if the speaker finds it easier to work back.
6. Humour, if required, planned to arise naturally from the subject-matter, not to be obvious or long-winded, not to be in 'chestnut' form and to be appropriate to the occasion and type of audience.
7. Quotations, if any, to be carefully selected for accuracy and appropriateness.
8. Speech now to be neatly summarized in briefest possible form – preferably on a postcard or series of postcards which may be studied unobtrusively.
9. Speech preferably tape-recorded if for important occasion; but at least heard by some objective critic. Notes made of suggestions for improvement.
10. Speech to be well rehearsed before formal delivery.

USING THE REFERENCE LIBRARY

Most towns have a good reference library which is used by only a fraction of those entitled to do so. A good reference library is a great help to the public speaker. It enables him to get information readily. If, for example, you wish to quote important figures or facts, or confirm or disprove the incidence of lung cancer in men under forty, or the imports of Spanish wines for the last five years, you will find this information in the *Annual Abstract of Statistics,* or in the *Board of Trade Journal,* which can be seen in the reference library. The assistants in these libraries are most helpful, and will go to a great deal of trouble to find out facts for you.

The *Encyclopaedia Britannica* is another valuable source of information which may be consulted in the Reference Library.

HOME REFERENCE LIBRARY

Every public speaker needs some kind of home reference that is immediately accessible. The content of this will vary according to your specialist interests, but the following books will always be found worth having at hand:

A good and up-to-date dictionary.
Fowler's Modern English Usage.
A good book of quotations.
A good encyclopaedia.
Roget's *Thesaurus of English Words and Phrases.*
Whitaker's Almanack.
The Daily Mail Year Book.
The Oxford Book of English Prose.
The Oxford Book of English Verse.
The Bible Designed to be Read as Literature.
The Complete works of William Shakespeare.
Makers of the Realm – Arthur Byrant.
A Writer's Notebook – Somerset Maugham.

Basic Psychology – J. S. Ross.

An up-to-date World Atlas.

Anthology of British Historical Speeches and Orations. (Everyman Library.)

Demosthenes, Select Orations. (Everyman Library.)

MAGAZINE AND NEWSPAPER REFERENCE

It is very useful to compile your own reference of articles and paragraphs cut from magazines and newspapers, filed under general headings, either in large manilla envelopes, or in files of thin cardboard with a spring back. An at-random search through a pile of recent popular magazines has turned up interesting and useful articles on:

The Origin of and Early Agreements concerning the Suez Canal.

Life in the Hebrides.

The Work of Somerset House.

A Guide to Careers.

Television for Traffic Control.

The Falkland Islands Dependencies Survey.

A Doctor in the Himalayas.

Profile of Rudyard Kipling.

Political Conventions in America.

From time to time articles are published on aspects of speech and voice production, choice of words, psychology of speaking and allied subjects, that are extremely useful. All these should be carefully filed for future reference. They will save you much trouble later and provide a first-class source of useful information. It only takes a few minutes now and then in the week to keep your home reference up-to-date.

A HOME QUOTATIONS REGISTER

It is not only the remarks of the famous that we may like to preserve and quote. Most of us say something wise occasionally and a useful register of such quotations can be built up at home, under an index system, in a book or on small cards. The following is an example:

Criticism
> 'He has the right to criticize who has the heart to help.' Abraham Lincoln.

Crooning
> 'Nowadays whatever is not worth saying is sung!' *Philadelphia Daily News*.

Dancing
> 'Dancing is wonderful training for girls. It's the only way they learn to guess what a man is going to do before he does it!' Christopher Morley.

Deception
> 'Women do things for appearance for which used-car dealers would go to jail!' Anonymous.

It is always irritating not to be able to remember a useful quotation. This is a great help.

LITERARY NEWSPAPERS

The term 'literary' is used here to distinguish these newspapers from the kind that is marked by sensational journalism.

The following newspapers are worth studying for the excellence of their articles on foreign affairs and on literature and drama:

> *The Times*.
> *The Guardian*.
> *The Observer*.
> *The Sunday Times*.

If your interest is in politics you should buy newspapers from *both* sides of the fence. You cannot refute what the rival party is claiming if you don't know what it is.

THE BBC

There are many interesting talks on the BBC Home Service from time to time; but it is the Third Programme that is the best value here. The idea sometimes expressed that the Third Programme is only for 'highbrows' is unfair. There *are* some rather 'advanced' talks; but in one week recently one had a choice of talks which included:

> The Towns of the Copperbelt (S. Africa).
> The New German Army.
> Industrial Design and the Common User.
> New Ideas in British Architecture.
> Restrictive Practices and Fair Trade.

The best of these weekly talks are reprinted in *The Listener* and are worth keeping in a Reference File.

Now here is a 'Quiz' with which to test your own background knowledge:

DO YOU KNOW THE ANSWER?

1. What were the main political events in the years preceding the outbreak of the 1939–45 war?

2. What, broadly speaking, is the work of the United Nations Organization?

3. Can you name all the British Dominions, Colonies, and Protectorates, and mention at least one of the leading political figures in each case?

4. What are the main differences in the systems of government of Britain and the United States of America?

5. How, briefly, would you explain to a visitor to this country the origin and function of (*a*) the House of Lords, (*b*) the Coroner's Court?

6. Can you explain the substance and purpose of the Bantu Education Act?

7. Could you say what are the main lines of argument used by those for and against the Partition of Ireland?

8. How did Trades Unionism originate in this country?

9. What do we mean by a Constitutional Monarchy?

10. Could you explain very simply the system of trial-by-jury?

11. Can you say when and by whom it was once proposed to extend British citizenship to an entire foreign people?

12. Could you compare in broad terms 'The Christian Doctrine of the Trinity' and 'The Islamic Doctrine of Kismet'?

13. Can you name four categories of people who are not legally entitled to vote in Britain?

14. Could you explain what is meant by the term 'Free Trade' and what political party favours it?

15. Name three political writers (who need not themselves be British) who you think have had the greatest influence on political thought in Britain in this century.

16. Do you understand what the Roman Catholic Faith maintains in the Doctrine of Transubstantiation?

17. Do you understand the significance of the Feast of the Passover to a member of the Jewish faith?

18. Could you trace in simple terms the influence of John Wesley on religious thought in Britain?

19. Could you state clearly what *you* understand by the terms:

(*a*) Marxist Communism, (*b*) Liberalism, (*c*) Democracy?

20. Could you give 'potted' biographies of each of the following:

(*a*) Robert Owen, (*b*) Albert Schweitzer, (*c*) Viscount Nuffield, (*d*) William Morris, (*e*) Madame Curie?

The following exercises are suggested for widening the scope of your public speaking. When you have worked through them you may care to invent more on similar lines.

MORE EXERCISES IN PUBLIC SPEAKING

1. You are the Warden of a Youth Hostel. This afternoon a party of young people from Hungary is arriving. They will be tired and hungry on arrival. After you have fed them make a short speech of welcome. They understand English but are weak on idiom.

2. You are a guest at the annual dinner of the local Archaeological Association, but are not yourself an expert on the subject. Make a brief speech replying to the toast of 'The Visitors'.

3. 'Poetry serves no useful purpose.' Please discuss this statement objectively.

4. You have been asked to talk to a Youth Club (mixed membership) on 'Choosing a Job'. Prepare a speech on these lines.

5. You are crippled from the waist down, but have surmounted this disability with courage and are a well-known designer (of what you please); give a talk to an audience of blind people on 'Living with our Lot'.

6. You have been asked to make a five-minute appeal for a charity. Please select your favourite charity and prepare a persuasive speech in its favour.

7. You are to open a Red Cross bazaar. Please prepare the appropriate speech.

8. Make a speech attacking thrift on the grounds that it is 'a cowardly virtue'. (Never mind whether you agree with the statement or not!)

9. Talk, briefly, to the children of a junior school (in the presence of the Headmaster and Staff), on the life of some great man.

10. 'The world owes the artist a living.' Please discuss the arguments for and against this statement.

11. Make a strongly persuasive speech for or against 'Total Abstention'.

12. You are the principal speaker in a Debate *against* the

Motion: 'This House holds that, not having asked to be born, man has a right to die when he chooses.' Make a speech on this subject.

13. The 'Hamelin Music Hall' has stood in your town for nearly a hundred years. It is now being pulled down to make way for a cinema. At the local Council meeting make a speech condemning this on the grounds that the 'Hall' should have been preserved for its historical value.

14. Explain the aims and rules of cricket to an audience of airmen at an American Base in this country (NB – DO NOT compare baseball with rounders!)

15. Make a 'Party Political Broadcast' in favour of any one of the following parties:

Communist – Conservative – Labour – Liberal.

16. You are a housewife who has been given the opportunity to talk to a gathering of industrial designers. State your criticisms of current domestic design; and your hopes for the future.

17. Make a speech proposing a toast to the visitors at the annual dinner of any organization you choose.

18. Make a short speech prior to presenting a gold watch to a colleague who is retiring.

19. You have been asked to 'say a few words' of a religious nature on the theme 'The Good Citizen' to a local church group. Please prepare this in simple terms.

20. You are the Manager of a local variety theatre. A famous film 'star' (choose your own) has been billed to make a personal appearance, but has failed, without explanation, to arrive. Make a conciliatory speech to a hostile audience.

21. Prepare and deliver brief *announcements* concerning:

(*a*) Facilities for the entertainment of the public in a newly-opened park;

(*b*) Collection of materials for salvage;

(*c*) Precautions to be taken (where you please) against an outbreak of food-poisoning which has not yet been localized.

22. Make a short speech to the members of your Club on the advice you would offer to beginners in public speaking.

23. Make a five-minute speech on 'The Advantages of Foreign Travel'.

24. Invent half a dozen colourful phrases you might use in the course of a speech on 'Sense of Humour'.

25. Make a very brief speech on 'Liberty' to an audience of long-term convicts!

PART TWO
FOR THE MORE EXPERIENCED SPEAKER

FOR THE MORE EXPERIENCED SPEAKER

The experienced speaker wishing to improve his standard must bear two important points in mind, intellectual content and style. There is no substitute for intelligence in a speech or, in fact, in anything else, and those who seek to disguise mediocrity by the use of cliches and pompous phrases deceive none but themselves. But even a speech of great intellectual quality can be spoiled by the style or mixture of styles in which it is delivered.

A speech is good when it conforms to the following pattern.

(a) It must say something worth saying.

(b) It must be free from verbal bluff of any kind, making its points with facility and directness.

(c) It must be so phrased as to seem original and interesting throughout and to be stamped with the personality of the speaker.

(d) At least parts of it must be memorable and quotable.

Style in spoken as in written English depends upon a choice of vocabulary and an ordering of words in a consistent manner so that unity – for better or for worse – is achieved. The style of *The Daily Mirror* is not the style of *The Times*; the musical style of Franz Lehar is not that of Mozart. Each is stamped by the impress of a consistent individuality. The style of today is, of course, far removed from that of the oratory of the nineteenth century. Gladstone's speeches though great of their kind and for their time would be unbearably heavy and tedious today; they had a ponderous strength depending upon a vocabulary of classical rather than of Anglo-Saxon origin and they took a long time to come to the point. Like the humour of the period, illustrated jokes in which four lines of dialogue had to have eight lines of explanation, they required time and patience for digestion.

The pace of living today obviates oratory of this kind. Now we require terse, economical speeches (though goodness knows we still get too many of the other kind) not without style but certainly without padding or ambiguity.

Here is an excerpt from a speech by Jawaharlal Nehru at his trial for sedition in 1940.

I stand before you, sir, as an individual being tried for certain offences against the State. You are a symbol of that State. But I am something more than an individual also; I, too, am a symbol at the present moment, a symbol of Indian nationalism, resolved to break away from the British Empire and achieve the independence of India.

It is not me that you are seeking to judge and condemn, but rather the hundreds of millions of the people of India, and that is a large task even for a proud Empire.

Perhaps it may be that, although I am standing before you on my trial, it is the British Empire itself that is on its trial before the bar of the world. There are more powerful forces at work in the world today than courts of law; there are elemental urges for freedom and food and security which are moving vast masses of people, and history is being moulded by them. The future recorder of this history might well say that in the hour of supreme trial the Government of Britain and the people of Britain failed because they could not adapt themselves to a changing world. He may muse over the fate of empires which have always fallen because of this weakness and call it destiny. Certain causes inevitably produce certain results. We know the causes; the results are inexorably in their train.

It is a small matter to me what happens to me in this trial or subsequently. Individuals count for little; they come and go, as I shall go when my time is up. Seven times I have been tried and convicted by British authority in India, and many years of my life lie buried within prison walls. An eighth time or a ninth, and a few more years make little difference.

But it is no small matter what happens to India and her millions of sons and daughters. That is the issue before me, and that ultimately is the issue before you, sir. If the British Government imagines it can continue to exploit them and play about with them against their will, as it has done for so long in the past, then it is grievously mistaken. It has misjudged their present temper and read history in vain.

This speech is marked throughout by a dignity and restraint rarely found in the speeches of nationalists of any race. The vocabulary is admirably chosen, making its point with economy and yet without sacrificing the note of controlled emotion, the absolute determination behind the simple words. Indeed, in at least one phrase – 'many years of my life lie buried within prison walls' – the speech becomes blank verse. It might well serve as a model to experienced speakers anywhere. Note how cleverly the very humility and simplicity of the penultimate paragraph gives greater strength by contrast to the laconic threat of the ending.

The style of the oratory of any period is shaped inevitably by the prevailing style of its writing, for we are deeply influenced by what we read. Among semi-isolated and primitive communities such as are still to be found in parts of the United States of America, where the Holy Bible is still taken as an absolute authority in a way of living, the everyday speech of the citizens is strongly coloured by the vocabulary and literary style of the Authorized Version. Style, then, it will be seen, varies in speech as in writing with the prevailing fashion. This is, in fact, more noticeable in speech because spoken English employs colloquialisms more often than written English does. The public speaker will try always to match his vocabulary and style with that current in his day and not to confuse his speaking with a mixture of styles and vocabulary in which nothing seems to fit.

An important ingredient of style is the division made by the speaker of words into groups or units. Just as in writing you will see that one writer will use very short, terse sentences or even write in jerky phrases giving an urgent, staccato effect to his prose, while another will use long, literary sentences flowing smoothly to their conclusion, so the speaker will suit his style to the effect he wishes to achieve and to the audience he is addressing. Short, simple sentences are certainly best for an audience whose vocabulary is limited by age or education; one would not use the same vocabulary in speaking to an audience of working men as one would use to an audience of undergraduates, though this should certainly not be taken to mean that one condescends to the former or flatters the latter.

The experienced speaker has usually developed a style and manner of his own by the time he can claim to be experienced. He is confident and fluent but the writer has noticed on many occasions that the most confident and experienced speakers often take the edge off an otherwise good speech by phrasing it badly so that the essential rhythm of speech is lost. It will be worth while looking for a moment at this question of phrasing.

First of all, let us be quite clear as to the nature and value of the neutral vowel in spoken English. To most of us the word vowel conjures up the five letters, a, e, i, o, and u that we use in writing; but the neutral vowel cannot be represented by one letter. Without using a phonetic symbol that would be unintelligible to many it can best be represented by 'uh'; it is, in fact, the little bleating noise that we all make from time to time when we are unable to think of the word we want. It is embodied in many words, such as 'pleasure', 'fountain', 'breakfast', and 'linger' and if it is not given its proper value in the pronunciation of a word it makes the word and the phrase in which the word is contained sound stilted and ridiculous. We do not say: 'I saw *ay* cat on *thee* roof.' We say: 'I saw *uh* cat on *thuh* roof.' Spoken as in the first instance the phrase sounds absurd, like an infant labouring finger-pinned over each separate word in a First Reader. Spoken as in the second example it has the natural flow and rhythm of English speech. Yet, even educated speakers in this country and even more so in the United States, insist upon pronouncing 'a' as 'ay' and 'the' as 'thee', thus spoiling the rhythmic value of their speech. 'The' must, of course, be pronounced as 'thee' when the succeeding word begins with a vowel. We should say 'Thee end' not 'thuh end'. The word 'and', too, is frequently given a false value. It is really only the sound 'nd; the 'a' is superfluous. We speak of bread'nd butter, of fish'n chips and this is not slovenly but rhythmic.

To prove for yourself the mangling effect of this failure to give the neutral vowel its proper value, read aloud the following short passage from the book of Genesis deliberately pronouncing the 'nds' and 'ands' and the 'thuh's' as 'thee's'; the moral will be obvious.

In the beginning God created the heaven and the earth. And the earth was without form, and void; and darkness was upon the face of the deep. And the spirit of God moved upon the face of the waters. And God said: Let there be light and there was light.

A phrase being a group of words belonging closely together it is clearly important that they should be kept together in speaking and not be divided unnaturally by breath-pauses in the middle. All speech has rhythm which is not to be confused with metre. Metre belongs to verse; it is the fixed beat depending upon accented and unaccented syllables. Prose is not metrical but rhythmic and the rhythmic style of its speaking depends to a great extent upon the facility with which it is phrased. In the following passage – again from the book of Genesis – the phrase-divisions are marked by a vertical line. If these divisions are made in the *middle* of the phrase the effect will be to destroy the lucidity and flow of the words as is unfortunately so often the case in churches where one would expect to find the highest regard for the meaning and beauty of the words.

And the flood was forty days upon the earth/and the waters increased and bare up the ark/and it was lift up above the earth.

And the waters prevailed and were increased greatly upon the earth/and the ark went upon the face of the waters.

And the waters prevailed exceedingly upon the earth/ and all the high hills that were under the whole heaven were covered.

Fifteen cubits upward did the waters prevail/and the mountains were covered.

And all flesh died that moved upon the earth/both of fowl and of cattle and of beast/and of every creeping thing that creepeth upon the earth/and every man.

All in whose nostrils was the breath of life/of all that was in the dry land, died.

And every living substance was destroyed which was upon the face of the ground/both man and cattle/and the creeping things/and the fowl of the heaven/and they were destroyed from the earth/and Noah only remained alive/ and they that were with him in the ark.

And the waters prevailed upon the earth an hundred and fifty days.

The experienced speaker should be capable of dealing easily with long phrases. If difficulty is experienced then more work on breath control is clearly needed.

During the course of examinations and adjudications I have often encountered students and competitors who have spoiled an otherwise competent performance by a failure to use pause intelligently. The experienced public speaker should have mastered this particular technique. Caesural and suspensive pauses are found only in verse and will not be needed by the public speaker unless he is given to quoting verse extensively, in which case he will do well to study the technique of verse speaking. Pauses for effect, however, are very much in the court of the public speaker. Not nearly enough attention is paid by public speakers to the use of pause for emphasis, for building up a climax and for highlighting a particular word. In the passage from Genesis recounting the story of the flood, for instance, there is the line: 'All in whose nostrils was the breath of life; of all that was in the dry land, died.' Here a pause between the words 'land' and 'died' adds enormously to the dramatic effect, greatly strengthening the verb. A slight pause before a rhetorical question also effectively highlights the answer. 'Why has the government taken this step against the advice of numerous experts on the subject?' demands the speaker. (PAUSE) 'because it is hypnotized by its own stubborn and unworkable policy . . . etc.'

The pause indicated above should not be held too long if only because a too-protracted pause is an invitation to the heckler The timing of a pause, as any actor knows, is difficult, largely intuitive. A well-timed pause can be so effective that the aspiring speaker will do well to study its use.

EMPHASIS

The emphatic quality of spoken English depends upon the recognition of strength in adjectives and verbs. The inexperienced speaker may encounter difficulty by failing to stress strong words altogether, by stressing relatively unimportant words instead or by firing a broadside on almost all words so that contrast is lost completely. Of these three faults the first is the most common. It is (together with failure to inflect) an error that leads inevitably to the most deadly vocal monotony. Let us consider an example from the works of Joseph Conrad:

And we *pumped*. And there was no break in the weather. The sea was *white* like a sheet of foam, like a cauldron of *boiling milk*; there was not a break in the clouds, no – not the size of a *man's hand* – no, not for so much as ten *seconds*. There was for us no *sky*, there were for us no *stars*, no *sun*, no *universe* – nothing but *angry* clouds

117

and an *infuriated* sea. We pumped watch and watch, for *dear life*, and it seemed to last for *months*, for *years*, for all *eternity*, as though we had been *dead* and gone to a *hell* for sailors.

In this extract some of the stressed words are nouns and these, too, are stressed because of their importance to the sense-structure of the passage. If the passage is read aloud without any stress at all it will be seen how much it is thereby weakened.

Exercise 1

Mark the stress-words and pauses in the following passage and practise reading it aloud:

In the name of the Third Reich free men and women were enslaved, tortured, and annihilated. The brave new German world that was to last a thousand years was founded upon the utter humiliation of the human soul, founded upon every kind of degradation and injustice. Its poisoned roots spread to every part of the free world where the goose-stepping jack-boots carried them and, in their evil spreading, they enmeshed all that was good, all that was free. In nothing was this more wicked than in the deliberate corruption of German youth. These children of God were taught to spit daily in the face of Christ, to inform upon their parents, to laud the virtues of brute force, cunning, and bad faith, to sneer at love and compassion, to brutalize all that they touched, to dwell constantly upon their supposed superiority, to twist the admirable loyalties of youth into a dedicated reverence for the diseased fraternity of their elders and to hurt and humilate not only those of the Jewish faith but all who were seen to live by humane and liberal beliefs.

What an eternity of separation from the love of God must these guilty men endure if 'suffer little children to come unto Me' is to have any meaning.

Exercise 2

The following passage is of quite a different nature and will be stressed differently. Prepare it for effective speaking as if it were part of a speech to be made to an amateur dramatic society.

The portrayal of a character upon the stage so that the person seen by the audience is wholly credible and, at the same time, a faithful reflection of the author's intentions, depends upon so many facets of dramatic art that it is difficult to know where best to begin.

The actor must persuade his imagination to range freely not only over those scenes in which his character appears, but also over the whole imaginary course of the character's life so that he is seen, as it were, in the round and his thoughts and actions are predictable in any situation.

The actor must live with his character as with an identical twin. It is not enough to move and speak mechanically as the producer directs. It is not, in the end, what the producer puts in that matters so much; it is what the actor brings out of himself, like ectoplasm. It may not be necessary ever to have been frozen and half-starved to portray an emaciated tramp but it is essential to be able to imagine how such an unfortunate feels and what effect his physical condition has upon his thoughts and ultimately upon his actions, if such a character is to be effectively acted.

The more an actor thinks round his part the more successful his characterization is likely to be. It is the imaginative thought that he brings to his task that colours and vitalizes his every word, his every movement, so that his art may finally project upon the stage a living, credible other-self rather than merely a costumed and painted puppet.

PHRASING AND BREATH-CONTROL IN MORE ADVANCED READING AND SPEAKING

The experienced speaker – and, in particular, he who proposes to enter for the advanced examination grades in public speaking, details of which are given separately in this book – must ensure his ability to deal with long phrases and a more complicated vocabulary than is normally used in less ambitious public speaking. Special attention should be paid to the use of the diaphragm in the control of breath and to this end, in addition to exercises for breathing alone, he should practise reading aloud from prose of a more advanced kind. The following is an excerpt from the Preface to *Man and Superman* by George Bernard Shaw. Apart from the interest of its content it provides an excellent exercise of this kind. Try reading it aloud, phrasing very smoothly and deliberately.

Among the friends to whom I have read this play in manuscript are some of our own sex who are shocked at the 'unscrupulousness', meaning the utter disregard of masculine fastidiousness, with which the woman pursues her purpose. It does not occur to them that if women were as fastidious as men, morally or physically, there would be an end of the race. Is there anything meaner than to throw necessary work upon other people and then disparage it as unworthy and indelicate? We laugh at the haughty American nation because it makes the Negro clean its boots and then proves the moral and physical inferiority of the Negro by the fact that he is a shoe-black; but we ourselves throw the whole drudgery of creation on one sex, and then imply that no female of any womanliness or delicacy would initiate any effort in that direction. There are no limits to male hypocrisy in this matter. No doubt there are moments when man's sexual immunities are made acutely humiliating to him. When the terrible moment of birth arrives, its supreme importance and its superhuman effort and peril, in which the father has no part, dwarf him into the meanest insignificance; he slinks out of the way of the humblest petticoat, happy if he be poor enough to be pushed out of the house to outface his ignominy by drunken rejoicings. But when the crisis is over he takes his revenge, swaggering as the breadwinner, and speaking of Woman's 'sphere' with condescension, even with chivalry as if the kitchen and the nursery were less important than the office in the city.

When preparing a passage for reading aloud it should be remembered that too careful attention should not be paid to every comma in the script. Commas are often present purely for a grammatical purpose and a slavish regard for them in speaking will often spoil the smoothness of the phrasing. This is illustrated in the lines above – '. . . its supreme importance and its superhuman effort and peril, *in which the father has no part,* dwarf him into the meanest insignificance'. The commas before and after the words 'in which the father has no part' are there for a purely grammatical purpose. In speaking they should be ignored for the sake of smooth phrasing. A *fractional* pause after the word 'part' may be necessary in order to get a clean attack upon the following verb, but certainly no formal recognition of the commas' existence should be made. Commonsense must be the guide in these matters. If the sense will in any way be impaired by neglecting a comma then it should be marked in speaking, otherwise it is best ignored.

It may be that the speaker is as yet unable to speak a long phrase without taking a fresh breath, in which case care must be taken that the necessary breath is snatched at the point where it will do the least possible damage to the phrasing. A quick breath of this kind should always be taken very rapidly and noiselessly through the open mouth, not through the nose. In this way it is possible to breathe in the course of a phrase without making a perceptible break and this is an art that should be cultivated by advanced speakers, though it is better still, of course, to strengthen the diaphragm so as to make the breath unnecessary.

CADENCE IN THE LONG SENTENCE

When a sentence is built up of a number of phrases, each following the other to a climax, it is necessary to inflect with great care. The final falling inflection comes at the point of climax and it will, therefore, be necessary to sustain an upward or level inflection on those phrases preceding the climax, otherwise the speech will sound like a series of false climaxes. Again an example from *Man and Superman*: 'Their imagination glows, their energies rise up at the idea of death, these people: they love it: and the more horrible it is the more they enjoy it.' In this short extract the inflections should be kept up until the climax on the final word 'it'. There will, of course, be some slight variation of inflection at the ends of the phrases preceding this but they are only the slightest changes in pitch.

Here, from J. B. Priestley's essay: *The Underground and the Future*, is a short excerpt which the reader may care to prepare for speaking, with due regard to cadence, marking the breathing spaces with a short vertical line and the rising and falling cadences with curved lines.

The other day I went by Hampstead Tube to Tottenham Court Road and changed there for Oxford Circus, and it happened that there were very few people about, so that I was able for once to think about my surroundings. At Tottenham Court Road I was carried up an escalator, went along a passage and down some steps, found another train that shot me into Oxford Circus Station, and there, after more corridors, I mounted an escalator so long and high that it might have been Jacob's Ladder itself. It was while I was being carried obliquely upward by this astonishing thing that I suddenly thought, I am a creature who is carried about in this fashion. There I was; I had said good-bye to daylight on the summit of Hampstead, had stepped into a little box that had rushed me down a shaft to some passages and a platform somewhere in the middle of the hill, had boarded a vehicle, a thing as terrifying as a thunderbolt, that had hurtled me under half London, and after that I had been going up and down moving staircases. I remembered that years ago I had read a fantastic story by Bulwer Lytton called *The Coming Race*, but that nothing in that story was as fantastic as this journey from Hampstead to Oxford Circus.

In the passage marked by a rule it will be seen that the inflections are kept up at the end of each phrase until the word 'corridors' has been spoken and, that if this is not observed and a falling cadence has been introduced, the sense of progression and continuity is lost and the reading thereby weakened in its impact.

Another example which needs the same careful attention to the rise and fall of the voice is the following extract from Jerome K. Jerome's *Three Men In A Boat*. It is a description of Moulsey Lock.

On a fine Sunday it presents this appearance nearly all day long, while, up the stream, and down the stream, lie, waiting their turn, outside the gates, long lines of still more boats; and boats are drawing near and passing away, so that the sunny river, from the Palace up to Hampton Church, is dotted and decked with yellow, and blue, and orange, and white, and red, and pink. All the inhabitants of Hampton and Moulsey dress themselves up in boating costume, and come and mouch round the lock with their dogs, and flirt, and smoke, and watch the boats, and, altogether, what with the caps and jackets of the men, the pretty coloured dresses of the women, the excited dogs, the moving boats, the white sails, the pleasant landscape, and the sparkling water, it is one of the gayest sights I know of this dull old London town.

This passage bristles with commas many of which – from an oral point of view – may be omitted, indeed, *must* be omitted if the phrasing is to be kept smoothly effective.

If, in music, a minim is played as if it were a semibreve the time-structure of the bar is distorted and the music accordingly spoiled and so it is in speech if words or parts of words are given an incorrect time-value. This is a more common error than might be supposed and the experienced speaker is no less likely to err in this respect than the beginner. Many speakers have a marked tendency to prolong unduly short sounds at the ends of words – 'dul*ee*' instead of 'duly', for example. Although there are always exceptions to any rule in English the following guide may be found useful:

1. The heavy beat is generally to be found at the beginning of a word: e.g. g*a*rden, w*a*king, pl*e*ntiful.

2. In multi-syllabic words the primary accent is found on the first or second syllable and the secondary accent on the fourth or fifth: e.g., s*i*nfully, imp*a*rti*a*lity, p*a*thol*o*gical.

3. Words ending in '-logy', '-pathy', '-tion', '-cracy' place the accent on the syllable just before the termination: e.g. phren*o*logy, s*y*mpathy, sens*a*tion, arist*o*cracy.

The rhythmic quality of oral English is impaired when letters or syllables are carelessly omitted as in 'prob'ly' for 'probably' or 'hist'ry' for 'history' though it should be remembered that the degree of care which should be taken in formal speech is not so important in ordinary conversation where over-careful stressing of sounds is apt to sound prim and pedantic.

THE BRIDGED HIATUS

The word 'hiatus' means a break or a gap and, in spoken English, to bridge this gap by transferring the final sound of one word to the beginning of the following word is to create an absurdity as, for example, to say 'bring i-tup' instead of 'bring it up'. There should be a hiatus, you see, between the 't' and the 'u'. Other examples of words which invite a bridging of the hiatus are:

(*a*) Bring it on.   (*d*) Here is a red apple.
(*b*) Take it out.   (*e*) I went in.
(*c*) He went up to Jerusalem.   (*f*) The coat quickly wore out.

PRONUNCIATION

It will be found helpful to scan a good dictionary now and then for words infrequently encountered and to note where the syllable stress is placed. It may save some embarrassment later on a public occasion. The following words are very often mispronounced. Look them up in a dictionary and make a note of the stress points:

Exquisite	Applicable
Despicable	Romance
Municipal	Incomparable
Controversy	Jewelled
Violence	Address

While slovenly speech is never excusable in any educated person care should be taken not to allow precision to fall into pedantry and, in this respect, we should consider carefully groups of words where one word ends with a consonant and the following word begins with the same consonant, e.g., 'about time'. Now, in this case, if a definite break is made between the two 't's an effect of primness is given and the phrasing is spoiled, so we must sacrifice the 't' in 'about' in order to accentuate the 't' in time. Other examples are: 'he spoke cannily', 'we're ready', 'a broken nail', 'the split top'.

EXAMINATIONS

One of the most important ways in which one can measure one's progress in any particular field of study is by submitting oneself to a written or oral examination and in nothing else is this more useful than in the field of oral English, which embraces elocution (in the best sense of that much-maligned word), reading aloud, acting, and public speaking. Examinations which are carefully graded in difficulty, extensive in scope and interesting in content help the candidate to progress more easily and to measure the degree of his own competence, leading in the end, if he so wishes, to a Diploma which is a guarantee of a professional standard, is not easily won but is well worth the winning.

A *new* series of examinations by the London Academy of Music and Dramatic Art (in addition to the Speaking and Reading Examination) begins – under the title Spoken English – with a Introductory Test for young children and continues through grades 1 to 5 and ends with a special Certificate of Merit. The Grade examinations are open to candidates of all ages and are invaluable in themselves. They include (a) Conversation, (b) Prose-Reading Aloud, (c) Story-Telling and (d) The giving of Prepared Talks on own-choice subjects. This series provides an invaluable 'run-up' to the more exacting Medal Examinations in Public Speaking. A quotation from the syllabus may be found helpful:

> The standard aimed at is a practical rather than an academic one. It is hoped to develop the kind of ability which enables people to make a favourable impression at an interview, when called upon to express an opinion at a meeting, or when asked to talk on a subject of which they have special knowledge ... Clear thinking, simplicity of expression, sincerity and self-confidence, are considered primary virtues. Humour and originality of thought and expression are to be encouraged but not forced ... visual aids can be taken into the examination room if required. Foreigners who wish to gain a certificate for their proficiency in English may enter for these examinations. They too will be expected to speak the language clearly and correctly but will not be debarred from success by their accent, as long as they are easily comprehensible.

THE BRONZE, SILVER AND GOLD MEDAL EXAMINATIONS
IN PUBLIC SPEAKING

These examinations are not open to candidates *under* the ages of (respectively) sixteen, seventeen and eighteen years of age. Candidates who have gained the Gold Medal in Public Speaking may then attempt the final Associate Diploma (ALAM) which demands a very high standard of competence.

Bronze Medal (Total time allowance 20 minutes)

The candidate to prepare and deliver two contrasting speeches, not to exceed four minutes each, on subjects chosen by the candidate.

To make an impromptu speech, limited to three minutes, on a subject to be given before the examination.

	Marks		
Voice	30		
Diction	30		
Deportment and grooming	15		
Prepared speech 1.	25		
„ „ 2.	25	Pass	110
Impromptu speech	25	Honours	130
	150		

Silver Medal (Total time allowance 20 minutes)

The candidate to prepare and deliver two contrasting speeches, not to exceed four minutes each, on subjects chosen by the candidate.

To make an impromptu speech, limited to three minutes, on a subject to be given before the examination.

	Marks
Voice	30
Diction	30
Deportment, etc.	15

Prepared speech 1.	25		
" " 2.	25	Pass	110
Impromptu speech	25	Honours	130
	150		

Gold Medal (Total time allowance 30 minutes)
NOT open to candidates under 18 years of age.

The candidate to prepare and deliver two contrasting speeches, not to exceed six minutes each, on subjects chosen by the candidate.

To make an impromptu speech, limited to four minutes, on a subject given before the examination.

To read at sight a test in prose.

To discuss the technique of Public Speaking and, at the discretion of the Examiners, points arising from the speeches.

	Marks		
Voice	30		
Diction	30		
Deportment and grooming	15		
Prepared speech 1.	15		
" " 2.	15		
Impromptu speech	15		
Sight reading	15	Pass	110
Discussion	15	Honours	130
	150		

THE DIPLOMA IN PUBLIC SPEAKING (Time allowance 1 hour)
(ALAM)

Before entering for this, candidates must have gained the LAMDA Gold Medal for Public Speaking. There are two examiners.

128

The candidate to prepare and deliver a speech, to *last* eight minutes, on one of the following subjects:

(*a*) Foreign travel – does it broaden the mind, or merely serve to confirm prejudices?

(*b*) One or two outstanding characters in English fiction.

(*c*) What plays might Shakespeare have written if he had been living in this age?

(*d*) 'A soft answer turneth away wrath – but grievous words stir up anger.'

(*e*) A notable eccentric.

(*f*) Humour as a weapon.

To make an impromptu speech, limited to five minutes, on a subject given before the examination.

To make a speech, limited to eight minutes, on a subject chosen by the candidate.

To read at sight a test in prose.

The candidate will also be expected to discuss with the Examiners the technique of Public Speaking and, at the discretion of the Examiners, points arising from the speeches.

	Marks		
Voice	30		
Diction	30		
Deportment and grooming	15		
Set speech	30		
Impromptu speech	30		
Own speech	20		
Sight reading	15	Pass	150
Discussion	20	Honours	175
Total	200		

The Guildhall School of Music and Drama also has a series of similar examinations under the title of Spoken English and

Speaking in Public, a new syllabus of which is to be prepared soon and which will embrace five Grade Examinations (Preliminary to Final) and a Diploma; but unfortunately details of these are not available yet. The minimum age for these examinations will be thirteen years of age. Full details may be obtained from the Examinations Administrator, The Guildhall School of Music and Drama, John Carpenter Street, Victoria Embankment, London, E.C.4.

Both of these Examining Institutions have Examination Centres widely spread over most of the principal cities and towns of the British Isles, and the Examining Staffs of both travel regularly to examine candidates at whatever centre is most convenient to them. For business people and others who find mid-week examinations impossible or inconvenient there are examinations held on Saturdays.

It should be stressed that the Examiners – men and women – are chosen not only for their professional competence, but also for their tact and ability to offer really constructive and helpful criticism to the candidate. This alone is reason enough for entering for examination, for we can obtain skilled help from these examiners that not even the best-meaning friend can offer. It is best to enter first for a Grade well within one's ability and to work steadily upwards from there so that a sense of continuity is established and progress is more easily measured. Details of fees and conditions of examination may be obtained from the Examinations Administrator, London Academy of Music and Dramatic Art, Tower House, Cromwell Road, London, S.W.5.

The following brief advice may be found useful by those deciding to enter for any of the above-mentioned examinations.

(a) Decide in plenty of time which Grade you propose to enter for.

(b) Prepare your work thoroughly. Slipshod work will waste your time and the examiner's.

(c) Do not think that, because there is a time limit of,

say, ten minutes, you have to pad out a speech to reach this limit. No examiner is impressed by irrelevant or repetitive material.

(d) Try to vary your speeches so that if one is serious in content the other may be lighter and with an unforced vein of humour.

(e) Use notes if you like but if you do make them small and unobtrusive. Notes must not be memorized and the speech delivered parrot-fashion. This is a certain road to failure.

(f) If you are preparing a speech with a political content please do not adopt an unfortunately all-too-common suspicion that, if the examiner happens to have opposing political views, you are foredoomed to failure. The examiner is not there to judge your political (or religious) views but to judge how you express them. His personal convictions do not enter into it at all.

(g) Remember that the examiner must decide in his mind how you would sound in a fair-sized hall, so project for distance and do not speak directly to him all the time. You should see an imaginary audience spread in front of you and use a varying eye-focus as if they were really there.

(h) If you 'dry up' do not lose your head or immediately anticipate failure. Examiners are human and know well enough what tricks nerves will play. They will be much more impressed if you get yourself out of it without making your temporary hiatus too obvious.

(i) Remember you may take your speeches in whatever order you choose. In general, it is wiser to end with the speech you feel most sure of; it is no harm to leave the examiner with a good impression.

(j) Do dress formally for your examination. You are not, of course, examined on your sartorial standard but an examiner naturally wishes to see you in all respects as you would be before an audience on a formal occasion.

(k) Stand well with head erect and without fidgeting.

(l) Your mark-sheet and the result of the examination

will be sent out a few minutes after the examination is concluded. The examiner is not permitted to discuss this with the candidate and his decision is final.

(*m*) All examinations of the London Academy except the Diploma may be taken at centres outside London.

PART THREE

SPEECH AND VOICE PRODUCTION

SPEECH

When you consider how deeply our spoken words can affect each other, and how easily we can be misunderstood in our simplest communications, it is odd that more attention is not paid to the elementary psychology of speech.

In the last twenty years or so we have seen the increasing importance and power of propaganda, not only in actual warfare but in that state of suspended hate called 'a cold war'. Even the everyday advertisement hoardings cry out the power of words in suggesting emotional states. Probably the simplest example is that wonderfully simple and effective advertisement which just says 'PLAYERS, PLEASE'. After the eye has been caught by that often enough, the words rise almost instinctively to the lips when we go to purchase tobacco, because we have been conditioned to think of that particular brand.

A MEANS OF COMMUNICATION

Speech is primarily a means of communication. Even animals have some means of 'speech' and can use different sounds to indicate fear, love, hate, and so on. Our language grows involuntarily – that is, we do not have to learn it as we have to learn a foreign tongue. We absorb our speech from the moment of our birth; it grows with us and is a part of our development. This has its disadvantages.

One of the greatest disadvantages is that we may take it altogether too casually because we have not had to take much trouble with it. The other is almost as bad. It is that we absorb what we hear whether it is good or bad; and it is bad more often than good.

The author's definition of 'good' and 'bad' speech will be given in more detail when the question of a standard speech is discussed; for the moment it will be sufficient to say that speech is obviously bad if it cannot be easily understood. It defeats the primary purpose of communication.

Now in childhood we are preoccupied with using the vocabulary we have acquired subconsciously, and with adding to it the new words that we are learning almost every day. We have no time for social preoccupation (perhaps prejudice would be a better word) and we see words only as means to the simple end of being understood. This is why a small child stamps with rage when adults cannot understand what he says. He is not angry because of the shape or colour of the words, but simply because they will not do his business for him.

As we grow older, however, all kinds of prejudices associated with words creep up on us. We come to label our fellows as 'good people' or 'bad people', as the right sort or the wrong sort, by the words they use and the way they speak them. This breeds fear. The fear of not knowing the right words, of being labelled inferior, of seeming stupid and uneducated.

Fear of this kind can drive people to do two unwise things. Either they may become aggressive about their speech and say; 'I know I speak badly and I don't care. What was good enough for my father is good enough for me.' Or they may copy what they think is good speech and not copy it properly, so that the speech they adopt is like an ill-fitting dress showing the rags beneath. This false gentility becomes a source of malicious amusement to their fellows.

The balanced individual sees speech as something better than this. He tries to speak clearly and naturally, not assuming a false character and not being content to speak ill if he can speak better. He sees speech not only as a means of simple communication but as an instrument of persuasion and beauty. He realizes that speech is the outward reflection of his inner self – a projection of his personality. He knows that if he has an idea worth sharing with his fellows, he must use the most persuasive medium he can to 'sell' his idea, whether for money or not.

George Bernard Shaw said: 'It is impossible for any Englishman to open his mouth without making some other Englishman hate or despise him.' When we are considering the social aspect of speech we must bear this in mind.

We should bear in mind also that distinctive kinds of pronunciation have a partisan significance too. Thus a man prides himself on speaking like 'a good Scot' or a 'good Yorkshireman', and so on. This kind of pride is easily wounded. A Yorkshireman may not mind your telling a funny story about a Yorkshireman; he may even forgive you for what you imagine to be a Yorkshire accent; but he is likely to be angry if you sneer at his way of speech. Regional susceptibilities are easily wounded.

It will be easier to understand the frustration we feel sometimes at other people's apparent stupidity, if we remember that the glib use of words does not always mean that we understand the ideas for which the words are merely a symbol. Some cynical fellow once said that if all the world spoke only on the subjects they were qualified to speak on, there would be a great and dignified silence! Certainly we all speak glibly on occasion about matters we are far from expert on. For this reason the public speaker should always examine well the content of his speech, to make sure that he does mean just what he says and not something quite or even a little different.

These word symbols describe two kinds of thing – the concrete object and the abstract idea. If we say 'umbrella' we are unlikely to be misunderstood. An umbrella is a clearly recognizable object with which all civilized people are acquainted. But if we speak of 'freedom' or 'inferiority' or any other symbol for an idea, a creature of the mind, we are in trouble at once, for although Smith is not likely to come to blows with Jones over the definition of an umbrella, he is quite likely to do so over the definition of abstract qualities such as these.

Tied up with the meanings of words is the effect of (in writing) their appearance, and in speech their rhythm and tone-colour or sound. Some words are fascinating in themselves, apart, that is, from their meaning. They have an attractive rhythm or they sound particularly musical. This makes them potentially stronger than their fellows because the hearers may be beguiled by these considerations at the expense of understanding the ideas they express. We all have our own favourites, but some of the following may be found attractive to most of us for one or both of the reasons advanced:

amber	memorial	tranquillity	lotus
fantasy	azure	orangery	preferential
demolition	courteous	turquoise	subtle
eloquent	epitaph	carnation	

If you examine this selection you will note two significant points. One is that there are a great many 's' and 'sh' sounds, and the other the frequency of the consonant 'l', which is the most liquid and beautiful consonant in the language. These are the sounds which soften and make fluid the most expressive and flexible tongue in the world.

Apart, then, from the mental images we raise by the use of words, we can influence our hearers by the musical quality of their production. This leads people to praise the softness of Irish speech, the singing lilt of Welsh, and the crispness of Scots articulation. Romance languages such as Italian and Spanish, having a profusion of open vowel sounds, are more musical in quality than guttural tongues such as German and Dutch.

These, then, are the considerations we must keep at the back of our minds when we are thinking of the effect of our speech upon others. If we understand how our audience is likely to be thinking, we can plan better the approach we shall use in 'selling' the ideas we wish to speak about, and we may avoid antagonizing them by some tactless remark.

An American writer said: 'A closed mouth gathers no feet!' but this is no good to us as public speakers. Our concern must be to think about speech rather more than most people since we shall use it more extensively.

138

CLASSIFICATION OF SPEECH

Spoken English falls into two main groups – evocative and factual. The first is the language of the poet, the writer and the orator. It is speech coloured with emotion. It aims to stir the imagination, to evoke memories, to play upon pride and national sentiments. It is the language of Shakespeare and Milton.

Factual English is the language of the scientist, the *lingua franca* of commerce. Into this category fall the Chairman's Review of the Year's Trading and the biologist's Paper on Single-factor Mutations in Germ-plasma. It shuns emotion; it tries to present facts coldly and objectively. The aspiring public speaker will have to practise both kinds of speech.

Every student of public speaking should print the following motto boldly and hang it where it will catch his eye!

> NO PUBLIC SPEAKER CAN HOPE TO EXCEL UNTIL
> HE HAS ACQUIRED AN EXTENSIVE VOCABULARY AND
> HAS DISCIPLINED IT TO HIS USE.

THE FEAR OF FORGETTING

The fear of forgetting, of 'drying up' completely before an audience, is common to all but the most confident.

'When I was a beginner with a repertory company,' a famous actor said, 'I found myself, on the opening night of a Noël Coward play, uncertain of my lines in the final scene which takes place mainly at a breakfast table. Accordingly, I printed out my cue and speech lines in different colours, and hid the paper on the upstage side of the table, away from the audience. To my dismay, however, when I sat down, I found that the stage manager had removed my paper. My mind went completely blank. I heard voices and knew I should say something, but no words would come. Then pride came to my rescue and, sooner than make a fool of myself, I forced my brain to stop reeling and concentrate. The words came back at once. Speaking to a friend later I lamented making a fool of myself. "When was that?" he said. "Last act," I replied, "when I made that dreadful pause; everyone must have seen I was stuck." "Didn't notice a thing, old boy," my friend replied. Now, with experience, I know it isn't true that a blackout is inevitable sometime, nor is it a hundred years long when it comes. It only seems like that.'

In prepared speaking you are less likely to be stuck like this. But 'off the cuff' it is not uncommon to have a temporary stoppage. There are two ways of dealing with it when it comes. One is to stop dead, drop your jaw, turn white (or red, according to taste!) and, generally speaking, give an exhibition of helpless despair. With lightning perception the audience will appreciate that you have forgotten your words! The other way is to smile gentle and ask: 'I wonder if we might have a window open (or closed according to season); it is rather warm (or chilly), isn't it?' All the time thinking fast, but with an absolutely calm and confident expression. This will give you plenty of time in which to recover. There are many alternatives. You can develop a slight sniffle, and have a dignified blow, or you can break off, again with a pleasant smile, and say: 'I do hope you will tell me if I go too fast or if there is any question you would like answered now, while you think of it.' It doesn't matter much what you say, so long as nothing in your voice or manner gives the slightest hint that you have 'dried'.

The human brain is capable of rapid recovery from a momentary paralysis; but you must give it a chance by putting on an act. Every actor has to learn this. Even established players sometimes forget their lines (often, in fact, in plays that have been running for months); but they are professionals, and they have been taught never to let it show. If it happens to you, *don't panic*. It will come in a few seconds. Meantime put on an act of this kind. It will save you and the audience much embarrassment.

CLICHÉS AND HACKNEYED PHRASES

We may speak of these together as phrases which, by over-use, have become stale and slightly absurd. Like 'nice', they are the result of lazy thinking, the first phrases which enter the mind and which are accepted because it is easier to use them than to look for something better. When we say that tidiness was 'conspicuous by its absence' or that rudeness was 'the order of the day', we are using stale expressions, and our writing or speech will suffer. A very long list could be made of such phrases, and each of us have our pet dislikes; but the following may serve to remind readers of expressions to avoid:

> Leave no stone unturned,
> Explore every avenue,
> Be made the recipient of,
> Stands to reason,
> The cup that cheers, etc.,
> Leave severely alone,
> More sinned against than sinning,

More in sorrow than in anger,
Sleep the sleep of the just,
But that is another story,
The psychological moment,

and so on.

And let us not forget our old friend: 'Unaccustomed as I am to public speaking!'

The special language of the Civil Service is full of such stale phraseology, and commercial usage, too, has its own brand. Public speakers should have no use for them.

SLANG

The use of slang is a matter for common-sense. Purists who raise hands in horror at the idea of 'adulterating the language of Shakespeare' forget that the scope and flexibility of our tongue are the result of the constant borrowing and adaptation from other languages, and the incorporation of contemporary slang in each age, that has legitimized many words of doubtful birth. Words which today are regarded as crude and vulgar were in common usage among eighteenth-century gentry. Conversely, some of our present words, also in common use, would have shocked the Victorians, who would not call a limb anything so suggestive as a leg.

The constant use of colloquial speech or slang gives an immature sound to adult conversation. The use of such school-boy slang as 'wizzo' and 'supersonic' and the ubiquitous 'smashing' makes adult conversation sound absurd and child-ish. Slang *can* occasionally be most effective, and, *where it will be more effective than any more formal expression* by all means use it. If it does not meet this requirement it is better not used.

Understanding 'The Works'

In learning the use of expressive and virile English it is as well to study the outline, at least, of the mechanism which produces speech from a stream of air. The human voice is a wonderful and complex machine. Few of us have any real idea how it works.

The public speaker must bring the muscles controlling both breathing and speech under his absolute control. Let us see how it works first.

THE WAY SPEECH IS PRODUCED

In its simplest terms the voice is born of an impulse and a squeeze.

The impulse to speak sets the brain-cells to work ordering a sound. The muscles of the diaphragm (which is the floor of the chest) and the muscles between the lower ribs exert pressure on the lung, and sends a stream of air up the windpipe. This is *just* air; until it reaches the larynx, or voice-box, it is soundless. Now the air passes through the gap between the vocal cords, causing them to vibrate and produce a musical note. The sound is without form, not having yet been made into speech, and is a small one. It would be hard to hear if we could listen to it at this point.

It has not yet been amplified. Now the sound passes on to the part of the throat just above the larynx (or 'Adam's apple'); this is called the pharynx. This is the first of the resonating cavities which makes the voice bigger. If you place your finger and thumb lightly on the throat at this point and swallow hard, you will feel the throat expanding between them. This expansion increases the space and allows the voice to 'stretch itself' and grow. On the sound goes until it reaches a 'cul-de-sac' and can go no further in the same direction. It has to make a right-angled bend in order to reach the mouth.

A famous teacher of singing, Manuel Garcia, said that his only complaint with Nature's management of the organs of sound was with the positioning of the mouth. This, he maintained, should have been on top of the head; then the sound could continue its upward journey without interruption!

It is this bend which causes so much trouble. If there is any constriction of the muscles controlling the opening of the throat at the back of the mouth, the sound is pinched and squeezed out of shape by the time it leaves the speaker or singer. This is why it is so vitally important to achieve relaxation of *all* the muscles of the upper torso, because they act in sympathy with one another, and tension in one spot is passed on to another.

Before we accompany the sound on its way, let us have a look at the structure of the mouth. (A small mirror will be useful here.)

If you poke your finger up behind the upper row of teeth you will find that the roof of the mouth at this point is hard and bony. This is called the 'hard palate'. Moving the finger backwards, you find that the roof becomes soft and fleshy and smooth and ends with a fleshy pendant almost like a tonsil, dangling in the middle of the throat-arch. This pendant is called the uvula, and we shall learn more about it in a moment.

You will have noticed, in some churches, a wooden board placed above the pulpit, so that the preacher's voice shall be projected off this board into the body of the church. The hard palate is there for a similar reason; it is the sounding-board of the voice.

Now the soft palate is muscular and is capable of being lengthened or shortened at will, and of being raised or dropped. It is, in fact, a door which can descend and close the opening of the throat completely so that the sound is driven upwards into the nasal passages and sinuses instead. This happens every time we make the sounds 'm', 'n', or 'ng'. It also, being soft, absorbs excessive vibration in the sound passing over it, thereby acting, too, as a softener.

The uvula also descends with the soft palate and plays its part in the 'shutting-off' process. You can test how this works by holding your nose tightly and saying the word 'king'. You will find that it is impossible to make the 'ng' ending so long as the nose is closed.

Now back to the sound on its way. It is projected round the bend, through the opening of the throat and into the cavern of the mouth, its next resonating cavity. Here it grows still bigger, not only by the resonating capacity of the mouth itself, but by sympathetic vibration set up in the nasal passages and sinuses and in the great cavity of the chest. But remember, it is still raw sound – no more.

Before we consider the shaping of the sound into speech we might take a look at an important aspect of the human voice. This is that it is a *self-tuning* instrument. Whereas one has to make careful adjustments in the tension of stringed instruments in order to achieve the required pitch, this is done as a reflex action by the voice, allowing one singer to reproduce exactly the pitch of another singer, or of an instrument. This is a wonderful and most delicate process.

The raw sound is next cut and shaped and rounded by the action of the glottis (at the back of the throat, producing guttural sounds), the tongue at all points, the teeth, the soft palate, and the lips. Once shaped and finished it is 'bounced' off the hard plate and projected into outer space.

The crispness of the voice depends upon the full use of the speech organs, principally the tongue, teeth, and lips, in making consonants which might be called the 'bones' of language. Upon the relaxation of the muscles and the control of the breath depends the tone-quality of the voice. Without this the vowel sounds cannot be produced freely, but are mangled, sounding harsh and unpleasant.

The larynx, or 'voice-box', is a delicate mechanism and, if subjected to prolonged misuse, it deteriorates rapidly. The orator who *blasts* his voice through the larynx, trying to make brute force do what should be done by skill, will soon have a husky, ineffective voice 'dead' in tone and quality; and which is unlikely ever to recover from the beating it has taken.

Beauty of tone is not a quality we expect to find in drill sergeants! But even they have had to learn to project the voice *on the breath* so that it may carry for great distances without leaving themselves speechless. Actors, too, learn to reach the back of the 'gods' by 'throwing' the voice without straining the larynx. If it were not so, they would never last a week in a large theatre.

WHY 'FUSS' ABOUT BREATH?

Students of speech and drama sometimes ask, petulantly: 'Why do I have to learn to breath "properly"? I've been breathing like this all my life; and I've got on all right with it!'

One can see the student's point. A fair question deserve a fair answer. The student was quite correct in saying he had got on all right with his breathing as it was; but what he overlooked was that, because A is equal to B it is not necessarily equal to C. The breath that is sufficient for one kind of speech may not do for another kind.

The amount and control of breath needed to lean across a table and say: 'Will you pass the mustard, please?' is negligible; the amount of breath necessary to have a close-quarters conversation with a friend is also negligible: but the amount and control of breath necessary to fill a theatre or hall are entirely another matter. It is, in fact, considerable.

Yet, it is more the control than the amount that matters. Look for a moment at the following test sentence:

NONE BUT THE BRAVE DESERVES THE FAIR

Now take a deep breath, blow most of it away and, with the remainder, repeat that sentence at an even pace. You can do it easily on little more than a whiff of air. Now take a good, deep breath again. Gobble the air in, pack yourself with air like a bullfrog and say the sentence. The result will almost certainly be windy and quite horrible, because you have taken in far more breath than was necessary and the excess got in the way of the tone.

We do not automatically adjust for breath, as we do for pitch; it is only by controlling the muscles of breathing and by experience that we can judge accurately how much we need for projected speech.

In its simplest terms the ideal is for the lungs to be filled up *from the base*; and for a steady fountain of air to be available when needed, so that the tone shall rise on a steadily ascending column of air which is squeezed at an even rate by the action of the diaphragm and the rib-muscles, and not blasted out by violent and unnecessary contractions. It may help to picture the voice as a tennis-ball balancing on a strong foundation of water representing the breath.

SOME EXERCISES TO HELP

First of all, find your diaphragm. Think of a skeleton and visualize the V shape in the middle where the ribs fall away on either side: the place where you are 'winded' if struck without warning.

Place your hand, palm-down, over this space. Now the muscle beneath your palm (the diaphragm) is, in a singer or trained speaker, active and powerful; but in your case it may be weak. Breathe in slowly and deeply through the nose *without raising your shoulders*; and see if you can feel the muscle moving under your hand, pressing it outwards. You quite probably cannot feel it. Never mind. This is quite usual. Try again and again and again. And concentrate on making that muscle move. Much of the control of muscle in any part of the body is the result of mental concentration. You must be patient. It will come in time.

Keeping your hand in that position, take a quick breath through the mouth and shout 'AHOY' loudly. *Now* did you feel the muscle working? If you did, that is good. But if all you felt was a strain in the throat, it is not good at all. You see, the diaphragm *should* allow you, by its action, to direct the shouted 'Ahoy' right from there and out with the minimum of interference. Try again, and this time *think* the 'Ahoy' from the depths. Forget your throat altogether. Regard it merely as a kind of drainpipe up which the sound will conveniently flow. When you have achieved this you will be astonished to find how far your 'Ahoy' can be heard without any strain on your part.

A less violent exercise for 'waking up' a sluggish diaphragm is sniffing. Imagine you have something that smells pleasant in the palm of your hand. Hold it up under your nose and take in a full breath in three sharp sniffs with a pause between each. SNIFF – pause – SNIFF – pause – SNIFF (Full). Hold the breath and then let it out silkily through the mouth, keeping the outgoing flow as steady as you can. At each sniff you should feel the little jerk of the diaphragm.

Before recommending any more exercises, let me make one point clear. If you do not feel the muscles responding as quickly as you think they should, *do not be discouraged*. You are not being a 'backward' student. Neither should you go on and on, getting more and more exasperated and achieving less and less. Five minutes night and morning, not worrying but thinking hard, will do wonders. You are almost certainly better than you imagine. Most students are. The only ones who fail to make progress are those who are too self-satisfied to think they need improvement and they are very much in the minority.

Now let us get the rib-swing under control. The upper ribs are attached to the sternum or breastbone and are immovable, but the six lower ribs on either side are attached only by means of cartilage, and they are capable of expanding to make more room for the expansion of the lung and, consequently, an increase in the air capacity. It is this increased capacity we are after.

Now place the palms of the hands on the extreme sides of the ribs with the shoulders held back but not stiffly. Let all the air out of the body. Now breathe in, as before, slowly and smoothly through the nose, and feel the ribs pushing outwards against the hands. When you are *comfortably* full hold the air while you count a silent three, then release it as before, slowly and smoothly through the open lips. It is important to emphasize the word 'comfortably' for the completed breath. Beginners sometimes fill up so much that they are positively blue around the gills with the effort; and this is unnecessary and, indeed, harmful if done often.

This exercise, done patiently and regularly, for not more than five minutes at a time, will enormously increase your lung capacity and help you with the impressive and well-projected speeches you are going to make later. And you *are* going to make speeches of this quality. Keep this in your mind and you will not fail. Willingness is all.

When preparing a script for speaking, it is a good idea to mark your *comfortable* breathing points with slight, red lines so that you may practise always breathing in the same place: and will not be caught midway through a phrase without enough air to finish it.

INCREASING THE RESONANCE IN THE VOICE

When we speak of a resonant voice, we are inclined to have in mind a rolling bass. This is because the lowest-pitched voices have a great deal of chest resonance, which is more obvious the lower the voice goes. But it is not necessary to be a bass, or even a baritone, in order to have a resonant voice. Lack of resonance is usually because full use is not being made of the resonating cavities of the head.

Take a slow, deep breath again. (Remember not to raise the shoulders. If you do you will be directing air into the shallow part of the upper lung and not into the broad base of the lung, which is where you want it.) Now release this as before, humming on a comfortable middle note. Iron out any jerks or gushes. The outgoing breath, *whatever* the exercise, must be satin-smooth. You can write this out and wear it on your heart! In a moment you are going to repeat this on a higher note – one whole tone up. Hit the next note right in the middle, and don't push. In the middle. Don't scoop up to it like a crooner. Now a note higher again, and continue higher each time until it begins to be uncomfortable. *Never* continue after this point. Start high and work down, not the reverse. This exercise should be worked through humming on 'm', or 'n' and finally on 'ng', in which latter the mouth will be kept loosely open so that the sound may get well into the nasal cavity. The soft palate will, of course, be in the dropped position.

Now an exercise for strengthening the soft palate itself. Repeat loudly and firmly the sounds OY-NG, OY-NG, OY-NG, holding the end for a couple of seconds each time. This should sound like the noise made by a large spring thrown violently on the ground. It is best practised away from the rest of the family!

Lack of resonance is often caused by rigidity in the muscles of the jaw, so that the voice is ground out of a constricted space and has no room in which to develop freedom and resonance. Tightness in the area of the jaw is sometimes the result of an accumulation of daily worries, often trivial; the 'setting' of the jaw is an unconscious reaction to them. The only cure is to be aware of the condition and practise dropping the jaw loosely, practise chewing as if you had an enormous piece of toffee or gum and were shifting it from side to side in your mouth; and practise neck-rolling to loosen the muscles of the neck and shoulders. Tension here will communicate itself to the jaw muscles and so to the intrinsic muscles controlling the tongue. Tension *anywhere* is a danger signal.

In the few nerve-racking minutes before you know you will be called on to speak – perhaps at an interview for a job – it will be found helpful in controlling the sick, hollow feeling one gets at such a time, to breathe in and out very slowly and deeply through the nose. You can do this without its being obvious to anyone, and it will help to bring the diaphragm under control, and so steady your speech.

We have been considering special kinds of speech – political, after-dinner, speaking to children, and so on – and now, while we are on the subject of voice and speech and how they work, it will be as well to clear up some definitions, among which are:

DIALECT, 'GOOD', 'BAD', AND 'STANDARD' SPEECH

First, dialect. This is described in the Oxford English Dictionary as a subordinate variety of a language with a distinguishable vocabulary, pronunciation or idioms. It is frequently confused with an accent, which is a manner of speech without a vocabulary of its own, and being recognized by distinctive vowel sounds and syllable stress. As far as the speaker is concerned, the difference is largely one of understanding. If a man says he is going to 'take a bath'; and he uses the short, flat vowel sound in 'bath', he may be speaking with any one of the accents of the Midland counties, but he will be understood by a native of any other county. If he uses the rounded vowel sound which sounds like 'bawth', he may be Cockney; but again he will be reasonably certain of being understood by anyone. Thus a speaker may be recognized *by his accent* as a native of Scotland or Wales or Ireland; he may be known as a Cockney, a West-Countryman or a 'Geordie': and still be understood with reasonable ease by anyone, so long as he speaks with an accent and not with a dialect.

To cite two examples:

1. You are sitting in a café in London. The man at the other end of the table leans over and says: 'Pawss 'u bu'er mite.' That is as near as it can be represented without phonetic symbols. He is a Cockney and he is trying to say: 'Pass the butter, mate.'

2. You have been drinking with a few friends in a pub somewhere in Northumberland. You walk towards the door. A local character, to whom you have stood a pint, says: 'Gannen yen mun?' *He* is trying to say: 'Are you going home, man?'

No difference seems, on the face of it, to distinguish either of these remarks. But there is a difference. In the first case the request, although it would defeat a foreigner, would be recognized as a Cockney *accent* by most Englishmen and its meaning would be divined after a momentary hesitation. In the second case, however, the first two words, at any rate, bear no resemblance to any word that might be encountered in literary English, and would be untranslatable by anyone who was a stranger to the district.

Now for 'Standard' English. This is where the fun begins, because *what* is standard English is hotly disputed. We have no time here for finer distinctions if they get in the way of the book's purpose, so for all practical purposes we will define 'Standard' English as that neutral speech which is to be heard by listeners to the BBC News programmes. It is the speech of the Announcers, and it seeks to be non-regional. You can recognize the speaker as an educated man, but you cannot say what is his home county.

Having defined dialect, accent, and 'standard' or neutral English, we now come to the troubled waters of 'good' and 'bad' English. You will remember, in the section dealing with the psychology of speech, we concluded that the association of speech patterns with class distinctions bred fear and dislike. We also took notice of the regional touchiness which makes a man declare that he is a blunt Yorkshireman and that he has no use for that lah-di-dah twaddle they talk down South, or which makes a southerner despise the 'uncouth and barbaric jargon' they speak in the North. To say nothing of the Welsh, Scots, and Irish, who all have their ideas on speech too!

This kind of 'over-the-fence' snapping will get us nowhere; it cannot define 'good' speech, however long it tries.

It can only aggravate regional prejudices on a 'My-Dad-can-lick-your-Dad' basis. Let us not waste time with it.

How, then, to define 'good' speech? We must come to *some* conclusion. Let us go back for a moment to the psychology of speech section and see if we can find an answer there.

'*The primary purpose of speech is communication.*' This is a statement that is hard to quarrel with. If I have an idea that I want to explain to you, I must do so either in mime or in speech, and speech is generally preferred. This takes us a step on the way, because we can now say that in order to communicate, the medium we use must be *readily understandable* to anyone we may wish to speak to.

'*Speech is a medium of persuasion.*' To get the best out of this we must not see persuasion in the logical sense only. I may persuade a man to drop a gun by the logical exposition of what society will do to him if he kills me; but I may also persuade him by playing on his sentiments and feelings in a way that has no relation to logic. How often do we hear the phrase: 'He talked me into it'? So speech, to be really effective, must have a persuasive quality that need not be dependent upon reason.

'English speech is diverse and flexible.'

This should read: 'English speech *at its best* is diverse and flexible.' The pedlars of 'nice' and 'smashing' know neither diversity nor flexibility. But at its best it is possible to convey exquisite shades of meaning in English.

If we summarize what we have agreed, we shall find that we have demanded three essential qualities from the spoken word that can be divorced from regional and national partisanship.

First: immediate comprehension.
Second: persuasive quality.
Third: ability to express fine shades of meaning.

If you agree with this you will see that the first quality does not ban the speaker with a regional accent, though it *does* ban the speaker with a dialect; the second quality does not ban the regional speaker, but, again, it bans dialect, since it's not the least bit of use being persuasive when no one knows what you are being persuasive about. The third quality bans no educated man, wherever he comes from. If he can use many words, he can make fine distinctions. Again, it is useless in the case of dialect because of its limited intelligibility.

We could now agree that a 'good' speaker has a speech that can be understood at once, that has a persuasive, musical quality, sustaining audience-attention, and which embraces a wide vocabulary so that meaning can be very clearly defined. Finally, we would mostly agree that the speaker's voice should be an unforced reflection of his personality. This debars the nauseating gentility of the social climber.

If the public speaker remains *himself* while striving for clarity and tone in his voice, he will be doing better than by allowing trivial distinctions to stand in the way of a speech which is interesting, sincere, and expert.

COMMON FAULTS AND THEIR CURE

SLURRING

The commonest enemy to intelligible speech is slurring, the running together of words or parts of words. Perhaps the pace of living today is responsible; at any rate, it is becoming more noticeable every year. The Transatlantic 'wanna' and 'gonna' are not quite naturalized here yet, but they have taken out the preliminary papers, and such slovenly noises as 'Init?' are natives of long standing.

Speakers who do not normally slur their speech sometimes do so in public speaking through a nervous desire to get it over and done with. This need not worry the beginner, so long as he is aware of the fault. It will cease as his confidence grows. It is the habitual slurring of speech that is really dangerous. This is due to mental and physical laziness – the line-of-least-resistance mentality.

It is not uncommon to hear an exasperated adult say: 'Open your mouth when you speak, child: I can't hear a word you say.' It is not, however, quite true that a wide-open mouth is necessary to clear speech, though there certainly should not be rigidity in the jaw. It is possible to speak quite clearly through a narrow mouth-opening. It is the back of the throat which must be opened wide. A lazy tongue causes most of the trouble; when this is allied to smothered production due to a partly-closed throat, the result is a mumble.

CONTROLLING THE TONGUE

If you say the sentence: 'What have you got in the bed?' you will see the importance of an active tongue, because it

154

could so easily have been rendered: 'Wa' 'ave you go' in the be'?' Remember, it is the vowels that give English its tonal beauty; but they must be held together with consonants, and these are, in *no less than eighteen cases,* made with some part of the *tongue,* either alone or in conjunction with the palate or the teeth.

The consonant 'l' is the most beautiful of all the consonants in the English language. It is a liquid sound and it is made by the pressure of the tongue against the upper teeth ridge. W. B. Yeats used this sound alliteratively when he wrote:

Lake water lapping with low sounds by the shore.

The consonant 'r' is made by the vibration of the tongue-tip against the hard palate, just behind the teeth-ridge.

Unless the tongue is active and controlled it is not possible to sound 'r' properly.

Exercises for the Tongue

(*a*) Say 'Lah-lah-lah-lah-lah' like this, rapidly, in sets of five.

(*b*) Repeat using: 'Lah-rah' in sets of five.

(*c*) Imitate a telephone bell – Breee-Breee! trilling the 'r' thoroughly.

(*d*) Memorize and practise the following:

> In Tooting, two tutors astute,
> Tried to toot to a Duke on a flute;
> But duets so gruelling
> End only in duelling,
> When tutors astute toot the flute!

LOW AND GLAMOROUS!

Women are the worst offenders in this respect. The fashion for film actresses (American) with voices of bass pitch and a quality just short of asthmatic has led many ordinary women to desire speech of the same calibre. Whatever may be thought about the glamour, the unnatural 'thrusting down' of the voice is exceedingly dangerous, leading to permanent damage to the larynx. A voice pitched up or down out of its natural compass is under strain; and strain is fatal. Ladies are recommended to leave their voices within their normal compass, and to concentrate instead on making the quality beautiful.

EXCESSIVELY HIGH PITCH

The social climber often has a voice of high pitch and shrill quality, blasted with gentility. This is designed to impress by its air of superiority. There is no cure except to stop climbing!

A more common cause of excessive high pitch, and one we can all experience, is nervous tension. Again women are the greater sufferers, because they tend to live more 'upon their nerves' than men do. This applies particularly to women in occupations such as teaching, which calls for the expenditure of much nervous energy. The strain mounts imperceptibly, until their voices have reached a dangerously high level. The voice *always* sharpens when fear, anxiety or anger are felt. The cure is (*a*) to be aware of the condition and (*b*) to practise relaxation exercises whenever you have a moment in private to do so. Teachers should 'pull up' occasionally and ask themselves if they have been speaking shrilly; if so, concentration on speaking softly and quietly will reduce the pressure on the voice and on the nerves. Those who have never taught numbers of young children can have no conception of the strain involved – a strain which has nothing to do with disciplinary difficulties: but arises from constant shifting of ground (mentally) to deal with the innumerable problems of a teacher's day.

NASAL SPEECH

Unpleasantly nasal speech is due to laziness of the soft palate and, in part, to uneven control of breath. The simplest exercise is to open the mouth wide and say, rapidly: 'ah-ng', 'ah-ng', 'ah-ng', as often as you can manage comfortably on one breath. Now vary it by saying 'oy-ng', 'oy-ng', 'oy-ng'. Next, alternate the two: 'ah-ng – oy-ng', etc. This invigorates the soft palate, stopping the sagging which leads to nasality. Again, this is best practised away from the rest of the family!

UNCONSCIOUS 'ER'S' AND 'AH'S'

These are the little bleating noises we make when we are searching for a word. It is an entirely unconscious habit, and most speakers, when reminded of it, are surprised and a little hurt. One student I had was indignant when told that fifty-three ticks had been marked against her, for each 'bleat' in a three-minute speech. It took a tape-recording to convince her. This habit can be eliminated by thinking out the sentence first and then speaking it, rather than beginning with half the idea and having to 'bleat' in the middle while you think of the rest. At first this will slow your delivery considerably, but the good habit will soon 'set', and you will recover normal pace. Another cure is to make a speech to a relation or friend who is prepared to make a tick for each bleat, and try each time to give the marker less work to do. It is important to get rid of bleating because it not only breaks up the rhythm of your speech, but it distracts your audience and becomes an accumulative irritation. It might even induce some sporting types to make a book on the number of bleats you would reach before sitting down!

INABILITY TO PRONOUNCE 'R'

In its extreme this inability causes the speaker to substitute 'w' for 'r'; but this condition is much less common than it used to be; and is, in any case, not difficult to cure. It is, however, quite common to find a speaker who either makes a Continental 'r', using the back of the tongue as a Frenchman does, or whose 'r' is feeble and untrilled. Don't imagine that every 'r' should be trilled. It is a characteristic of Scots speech, but not of English speech; and to over-trill is as bad as not to trill at all.

The virtual banishment of the consonant in the south of England is the subject of some controversy. Personally, I believe it to be unconditionally bad, robbing speech of virility.

To say: 'Leathah pouches are bettah than rubbah ones' is to emasculate a noble tongue. In addition, it sounds pompous.

If you have difficulty in sounding 'r' the following exercise will help you if you persevere with it; but it must be practised regularly if only for five minutes a day.

First, loosen the muscles by sticking the tongue out as far as it will go and moving it from side to side. Now move it up and down and in and out. Do this for about a minute.

Now say slowly the two sounds 'Ah' and 'Ge' making the latter soft, as in the word 'German'. Again, 'Ah . . . Ge'. You are going to repeat this in a moment. When you do, try to 'bound' straight from the 'ge' sound into a trilled 'r' by blowing hard on the tip of your tongue, thus:

$$Ah \ldots ge \; (r)$$

The 'ge' is a vocal spring-board from which to reach the 'r' position. You will probably take a long time to get this, depending on your mental concentration; but when you do you will then be able to sound a normal 'r' in any word.

LISPING

There are two kinds of lisp commonly met with. One substitutes 'th' for 's' – 'wathp' for 'wasp'. The other is the recurrence of an 'ssss' sound when other consonants are being formed, and this kind of lisp is usually the result of dental malocclusion, or leakage of sound due to gaps in the teeth. In children this is not too serious because a dentist can often deal with it or nature may do so by providing a second set of teeth. In adults it may be the result of ill-fitting dentures.

The substitution of 'th' can be corrected by exercise because it is only the result of an incorrect tongue position. To make 's' the tongue-tip should be drawn back from the upper teeth-ridge, the sides of the tongue touching the upper teeth, with a groove down the middle of the tongue, along which the breath passes over the tip as it comes out of the mouth.

When the faulty 'th' sound is made, it is because the tongue-tip instead of being behind the upper teeth-ridge, is placed *between* the teeth. The correct position can easily be practised with the aid of a mirror.

DRAWLING

Drawling is more than a habit – it is a vice. It does more than anything else to make speech monotonous and tiresome. Drawling is not a fault in the sense that inability to sound 'r' is a fault. There is no organic excuse for the drawler; he drawls because he prefers to speak that way. It may be the expression of an easy-going personality refusing to be hurried; but it is often an affectation which has become habitual. It can only be cured if the drawler realizes that it is spoiling his speech and determines to stop it. Drawling has a soporific effect upon an audience. A drawler has to be in other respects a brilliant speaker if he is to hold his audience's attention for ten minutes.

HOW TO IMPROVE YOUR DICTION

Many people react to the word 'elocution' with a shudder. This is a pity because elocution, in the sense of the expert and *natural* use of the organs of speech, is an excellent thing. Why the shudder? It is because the exponents of what is satirically called the 'How-Now-Brown-Cow' School have brought the word into disrepute. There are not many who teach this kind of affected prattle; but it was once fashionable. It was characterized by a tendency to angle the head appealingly, raise the eyebrows, roll the eyes, purse the lips like a goldfish feeding, and breathe out the speech like a rather sick sheep with a tendency to asthma. It was 'too too' sickeningly artificial and it did a good deal of harm.

Putting this absurd posturing firmly on one side, it is essential, if you wish your speech to be effective, that every word you say should be heard without effort by *all* your hearers. Nothing is more irritating than to only half hear a speaker, to catch his voice, as it were, in gusts. There is no short-cut, no six-easy-lessons technique to good diction, only constant practice, making the tongue muscles trip lightly along, and using teeth and lips in support.

Only hard work will give you first-class diction. The finest material in the world for practising this flexibility is the opera libretti of W. S. Gilbert. This is published – separately from the music – in a book called *The Savoy Operas* by Macmillan and Co., Limited, St Martin's Street, London, and it is a goldmine of brilliant satirical verse. The two short extracts below will give you an idea of its suitability for articulation practice.

The Major-General's Song from 'The Pirates of Penzance'

I am the very model of a modern Major-General,
I've information vegetable, animal, and mineral,
I know the kings of England and I quote the fights historical,
From Marathon to Waterloo in order categorical.
I'm very well acquainted, too, with matters mathematical,
I understand equations, both simple and quadratical,
About binomial theorem I'm teeming with a lot of news —
With many cheerful thoughts about the square on the hypotenuse.

and –

The Song of the Lord Chancellor from 'Iolanthe'

You're a regular wreck with a crick in your neck,
And no wonder you snore for your head's on the floor,
And you've needles and pins from your toes to your shins,
And your flesh is a-creep for your left leg's asleep,
And some fluff in your lung and a feverish tongue,
And a thirst that's intense and a general sense
That you haven't been sleeping in clover;
But the darkness has passed and it's daylight at last,
And the night has been long, ditto ditto my song,
And thank goodness they're both of them over!

When you can repeat these lyrics at speed without scamping a syllable, you can boast of your diction to anyone.

HOW TO RETAIN THE INTEREST
OF YOUR HEARERS

Apart from the content of your speech (which has been discussed in detail earlier) you can keep the attention of your hearers even with an indifferent subject-matter, if your speech presents an ever-changing pattern of pace, inflection, and tone-colour. A great actor or actress could make the fat-stock prices sound exciting by the use of a perfectly controlled and modulated voice. Whenever you speak try to keep in mind the determination to vary all these things constantly, giving your audience no straight lines to lull themselves to sleep with. To illustrate this, here is Iago's speech 'Put money in thy purse' from Shakespeare's *Othello*. It is a speech with a constantly-changing pattern as you will see.

First of all, let us get the background clear.

Roderigo, a foolish and wealthy young Venetian, covets Desdemona, the wife of Othello, the Moorish general whom Iago hates and plans to destroy. Iago has been accepting money and jewellery from Roderigo, who thinks that Iago is acting as matchmaker or, at any rate, confidant between Desdemona and himself. But Iago has kept the money and jewels and Desdemona – not even knowing of Roderigo's existence – has married Othello, and is to sail at once with him to Cyprus. Roderigo, in great despair, has said to Iago: 'I will incontinently drown myself!' Iago replies:

> It is merely a lust of the blood and a permission of the will. Come, be a man! Drown thyself! Drown cats and blind puppies.
>
> I have profest me thy friend, and I confess me knit to thy deserving with cables of perdurable toughness. I could never better stead thee than now. *Put money in thy purse*; follow thou the wars; defeat thy favour with an usurpt beard; *I say put money in thy purse*.
>
> It cannot be that Desdemona should long continue her love to the Moor – *put money in thy purse* – nor he his to

her: it was a violent commencement, and thou shalt see an answerable sequestration; *put but money in thy purse*.

These Moors are changeable in their wills; – *fill thy purse with money*; – the food that to him now is as luscious as locusts shall be to him shortly as bitter as coloquintida.

She must change for youth; when she is sated with his body she will find the error of her choice; she must have change; she must; therefore, put money in thy purse.

If thou wilt needs damn thyself do it a more delicate way than drowning. *Make all the money thou canst*: if sanctimony and a frail vow betwixt an erring barbarian and a super-subtle Venetian be not too hard for my wits and all the tribe of hell, thou shalt enjoy her; *therefore, make money*.

A pox o' drowning thyself! it is clean out of the way; seek thou rather to be hang'd in compassing thy joy than be drown'd and go without her.

Roderigo: Wilt thou be fast to my hopes if I depend on the issue?

Iago: Thou art sure of me: *go, make money*. I have told thee again and again, I hate the Moor: my cause is hearted: thine hath no less reason. Let us be conjunctive in our revenge against him: if thou canst cuckold him thou dost thyself a pleasure, me a sport.

There are many events in the womb of time, which will be deliver'd. Traverse; go; *provide thy money*.

We will have more of this tomorrow. Adieu.

Consider this as a piece of villainous persuasion. The leitmotif is the reiterated advice to *make money* and leave the rest to time. Roderigo, like most fools, is obstinate. See how cunningly and with what ever-changing pace and inflection Iago plays upon his hopes and fears, now coaxing, now snapping, but always encircling the confused Roderigo mentally and physically. The advice to make money is given each time with different tone-colour and inflection and at a different pace, now soothing and friendly, now bluff and hearty, but never the same.

All through the speech there are subtle changes of inflection indicating scorn, bluff honesty, sly persuasion, plain reason, frank optimism, 'give-me-patience', smooth reassurance, and gloating anticipation. It is a masterpiece.

USING A TAPE-RECORDER

Even if one does not wish to buy a tape-recorder, it is possible for a few shillings to hire one for an evening. What does the tape-recorder do that makes it so valuable? 'I can hear my own voice without a recording,' you may say. But that is just the point – you *can't*.

There are two good reasons why we cannot hear our own voices as they sound to others. The first is that what we hear ourselves comes to us mainly by vibration in the bones of the head, and by reflected sound, thrown back by solid objects it has encountered and which is slightly distorted on its return.

The second is that, to some extent, *we hear what we want to hear*. The girl who passionately wants to believe she speaks with the husky glamour of Gertrude Gush, the latest idol of the 'lunatic fringe', will *hear* that kind of voice when she speaks, although to others she may sound flat, suburban, and entirely uninteresting. We are not all as foolish as this, of course; but in lesser ways we are unwilling to hear what we don't want to hear, and ready to hear what we hope for.

The microphone will have none of this; and will, within narrow technical limits, reproduce us, for better or for worse, as we *are*.

The encouraging thing is that many of us are a great deal better than we imagine, for the inability to hear ourselves without recording apparatus can work in our favour as well. I have had many students whose opinion of their own voices was needlessly low; and who were greatly encouraged by a tape-recording.

Some, on the other hand, whose voices were quite well produced and came back clearly, were disappointed because, although they could see the good points, they had imagined something, not better, but *different*. 'I thought I had a deeper voice,' they said, or: 'I sound just like my sister.' After a time these students usually became accustomed to their recorded voices and, in the end, accepted them as they were quite happily.

The greatest value in a tape-recording lies in the way it helps you to appreciate weaknesses you would otherwise have missed. This is especially true of breathing troubles and monotony. Both of these faults are sometimes difficult to recognize without this aid. You don't *feel* any difficulty in breathing and so you do not realize that it is the distribution of your breath that is at fault; and you are too obsessed with your thoughts to realize that your expression of them is uninflected and dull. But you hear this immediately on the recording. To get the best out of a tape-recorder you must use it systematically and resist temptation to treat it like an amusing toy.

Suppose you have prepared a speech for an important occasion in a few days time; and you want to hear what it sounds like. You hire a tape-recorder for an evening. This may cost you about fifteen shillings and it will be worth every penny of it.

First, record the speech exactly as you will say it. Remember, don't read it – *speak it*. Now settle down in a comfortable armchair, relax and (having first rewound) play it back. Don't attempt to pick this fault or that fault with it; just get the general picture. Now have a notebook and pencil handy, or the script from which the speech was prepared; rewind and play it all back again. This time look for *one fault only*. I suggest you look for monotony of pace and of inflection and tick the places in the script where it was most noticeable. Now play it again and look for failure to mark climaxes and emphases, for repetitions and hemming and hawing and mark them in the script. Now play the whole thing over once more and see if you can pick out anything you missed previously.

When you have done this take a few 'dummy runs' through the revised script, and finally re-record the whole speech correcting as much as you can.

By this means you can completely transform an indifferent speech, improving it out of all recognition. Isn't that worth a few shillings?

If you have no special occasion to prepare for, but just want the clearest all-round picture you can get of your voice, I suggest the following routine:

Prepare in advance –

Two breathing and voice exercises as recommended in this book or from any other source you please.

A piece of weighty and resounding prose, such as that of Dr Johnson. *The Oxford Book of English Prose* will help.

Some light fiction such as part of one of the delightful short stories of Patrick Campbell. (See the *Phoenix Book of Wit and Humour*.)

A piece of poetry that *really moves you*.

A satirical poem such as 'Sarah Byng', from *Selected Cautionary Verses* by Hilaire Belloc.

A spontaneous speech of your own composition on any subject chosen for you by a relative or friend.

This should give you about twenty minutes of widely differing speech. Record this and play back, noting faults in a notebook as you do so.

A recording which only lasts a few minutes is not enough time in which to get a worthwhile impression of your speech. Try to have at least a quarter of an hour.

Whatever the playback may sound like, *don't let it discourage you*. YOU ARE HALF WAY TOWARDS CURING YOUR FAULTS WHEN YOU KNOW WHAT THEY ARE!

WORRIES ABOUT PRONUNCIATION

We sometimes encounter words that are new to us or that are part of a foreign language; and it is embarrassing not to be sure how they should be pronounced. It is best to use only English words when we can, and to keep those as short as possible – there is no virtue in using long words *because* they are long and might be thought impressive: much of the magnificent English of the Authorized Version is in words of great simplicity – but we are bound, sooner or later, to encounter unfamiliar words when we are reading and there is no avoiding them. The best way of preparing for that moment is to make a list of the words you have doubts about, and look them up in a good pronouncing dictionary. Often the mispronunciation is a matter of syllable-stress, as in the word 'exquisite' which is often (even, I regret to say, by the BBC) mispronounced 'ex*qui*site' with the accent on the second syllable instead of on the first. Here are some other words that are frequently mispronounced; if you are uncertain of any of them it will be as well to look them up.

discipline	tulip	literary
advertisement	inexplicably	seance
irreparable	poignant	feign
repetitive	February	crescendo
dour	violet	really
scion	dais	impotent
assay	particularly	physicist

The pronunciations of 'vylet' for 'violet' (making two syllables instead of three), 'reely' for 'really'; and 'Febuary' for 'February' are common. It is also common for 't' to be given the sound of 'ch' as in '*ch*ulip' for 'tulip'.

The names of foreign personalities are also a worry; and even the august BBC appears to have widely differing views on this. One announcer will refer to 'Mr Krooschoff' and another to 'Mr Krooscheff'; your guess is as good as mine!

FOREIGN EXPRESSIONS

Foreign expressions are seldom necessary or desirable in English speech. Even when you are sure of the pronunciation of a foreign expression it is better not to use it if you can think of an English word instead. The use of foreign expressions is common on the part of those delightfully pedantic oddities who occasionally blossom forth as literary or dramatic critics. 'It wanted more panache, I felt,' one will squeak in a desiccated falsetto. 'Why not say it could do with a little more swagger?' you ask. 'My dear fellow,' he squeals in horror, 'there is a subtle difference, you know, between panache as the French mean it, and swagger as we do.' He is right; but he is not addressing his critique to an audience all – or even many – of whom appreciate that there is a slight difference, and he is quite pained when you point this out to him.

This kind of verbal snobbery is best ignored. If you have something to say which cannot be said in plain English, it is not likely to be worth saying anyway.

However, if the pronunciation of commonly-encountered terms worries you, it is best to look them up and note the correct pronunciation for future use. A few to start with might help:

aide-de-camp	coiffure	vis-à-vis
coup d'état	bourgeois	viva-voce
faux-pas	contretemps	buffet
hors d'oeuvre	gauche	naïve

Where a foreign word is commonly anglicized, do not be afraid to do so because you may be thought ignorant. If we were to pronounce 'café' as a Frenchman pronounces it, we would sound silly and affected.

TWO SPEECHES FOR ANALYSIS
AND PRACTICE

Here are two speeches in contrasting styles of oratory. It will be found useful to analyse them and prepare them for delivery in the light of the advice given throughout this book. The first is an extract from a long speech of The Devil from George Bernard Shaw's *Man and Superman*:

THE DEVIL: '... There is nothing in Man's industrial machinery but his greed and sloth: his heart is in his weapons. This marvellous force of life of which you boast is a force of Death: Man measures his strength by his destructiveness. What is his religion? An excuse for hating me. What is his law? An excuse for hanging you. What is his morality? Gentility! an excuse for consuming without producing. What is his art? An excuse for gloating over pictures of slaughter. What are his politics? Either the worship of a despot because a despot can kill, or parliamentary cock-fighting.

'I spent an evening lately in a certain celebrated legislature, and heard the pot lecturing the kettle for its blackness, and ministers answering questions. When I left I chalked up on the door the old nursery saying: "Ask no questions and you will be told no lies". I bought a sixpenny family magazine, and found it full of pictures of young men shooting and stabbing one another. I saw a man die: he was a London bricklayer's labourer with seven children. He left seventeen pounds club money; and his wife spent it all on his funeral and went into the workhouse with the children next day. She would not have spent sevenpence on her children's schooling: the law had to force her to let them be taught gratuitously; but on death she spent all she had. Their imagination glows, their energies rise up at the idea of death, these people: they love it, and the more horrible it is the more they enjoy it. Hell is a place far above their comprehension: they derive their notion of it from two of the greatest fools that ever lived, an Italian and an Englishman. The Italian described it as a place of mud, filth, frost, fire, and venomous serpents: all torture. This ass, when he was not lying about me, was maundering about some woman whom he saw once in the street. The Englishman described me as being expelled from heaven by cannons and gunpowder; and to this day every Briton believes that the whole of his silly story is in the Bible. What else he says I do not know: for it is all in a long poem which neither I nor anyone else ever succeeded in wading through.

'It is the same in everything. The highest form of literature is the tragedy, a play in which everybody is murdered at the end. . . . I could give you a thousand instances; but they all come to the same thing: the power that governs the earth is not the power of Life but of Death; and the inner need that has served Life to the effort of organizing itself into the human being is not the need for higher life but for a more efficient engine of destruction.'

Next, part of a speech by The Herald from *The Agamemnon* of Aeschylus.

'The rolling years have given all things a prosperous end, though some were hard to bear: for who, not being a god, can hope to live long years of bliss unbroken?

'A weary tale it were to tell the tithe of all our hardships; toils by day and night, harsh harbourage, hard hammocks and scant sleep. No sun without new troubles and new groans shone on our voyage.

'And when, at last, we landed our woes were doubled. 'Neath the hostile walls, on marshy meads night-sprinkled by dews, we slept, our clothes rotted with drenching rain, and like wild beasts, with shaggy, knotted hair.

'Why should I tell bird-killing winter's sorrows, long months of suffering from Idean snows, then summer's scorching heat, when noon beheld the waveless sea beneath the windless air in sleep diffused? These toils have run their hour; the dead care not to rise; their roll our grief would muster o'er in vain; and we who live vainly shall fret at the cross strokes of fate.

'Henceforth, to each harsh memory of the past, farewell!

'We who survive this long-drawn war have gains to count that far outweigh the loss. Well may we boast in the face of the shining sun: o'er land and sea our winged tidings wafting.

'THE ACHEAN HOST HATH *CAPTURED TROY*!

'And now, on the high temples of the gods we hang these spoils, a shining grace there to remain our heritage for ever.

'These things to hear shall men rejoice, and with fair praises laud the State and its great generals, laud the grace of Jove, the Consummator!

'I have said.'

I began this book with a quotation, and I should like to end it with one that I believe we should all learn and respect:

Success, for any sane adult, is exactly equivalent to doing his best. What that best may be, what its farthest reaches may include, we can discover *only by freeing ourselves from the will to fail.*

(Dorothea Brand)

Good luck!

A Multilingual Commercial Dictionary
£1.95

Some 3,000 words and phrases in common commercial use
are listed in English, French, German, Spanish and Portuguese
followed by their translation in the other languages. The
equivalent American expression is also included where relevant.
Simple to use and invaluable for everyday reference, the
dictionary covers terms used throughout banking, accounting
insurance, shipping, export and import and international trade.

edited by A. L. Bacharach and J. R. Pearce
The Musical Companion £3.50

The classic musical reference book, first published in 1934
and a steady bestseller ever since ; now thoroughly revised and
up-dated for the world of music today — instruments of the
orchestra — opera — the human voice — chamber music — the
solo instrument — listening and performing. Contributors include
David Atherton, Eric Blom, Alan Blyth, Hugo Cole,
Edward J. Dent, Robert Layton, John McCabe, Charles
Osborne, Francis Toye, and many more.

'The most useful, comprehensive and popular introduction
to its vast subject' DESMOND SHAWE-TAYLOR

Dr Shewell-Cooper's Basic Book of Weekend Gardening £1.25

A month-by-month guide to gardening throughout the year
which is designed to help those gardeners with only limited
time to spare. Dr W. E. Shewell-Cooper, one of Britain's best-
known gardening writers, covers all the tasks and pitfalls likely
to occur in the average year in this ideal companion for the weekend
gardener.

Peter F. Drucker
Management £2.50

Peter Druker's aim in this major book is 'to prepare today's and tomorrow's managers for performance. He presents his philosophy of management, refined as a craft with specific skills: decision making, communication, control and measurement, analysis — skills essential for effective and responsible management in the late twentieth century.

'Crisp, often arresting . . . A host of stories and case histories from Sears Roebuck, Marks and Spencer, IBM, Siemens, Mitsubishi and other modern giants lend colour and credibility to the points he makes' THE ECONOMIST

C. Northcote Parkinson and Nigel Rowe
Communicate £1.25
— Parkinson's formula for business survival

Peter Druker says in his foreword: 'This book, to my knowledge, for the first time, tackles all four elements of communication (what to say; when to say it; whom to say it to; how to say it). It makes the businessman literate and it gives him the competence which he needs.'

'Will be read avidly by the professionals and the amateurs in PR, but it is the individual businessman who will gain most from it' THE DIRECTOR

Alastair Mant
The Rise and Fall of the British Manager £1.20

'Seeks to explain, in a vigorous style, why in this country we "downgrade so many of the jobs that really matter" . . . Mant argues that the business of making and selling things, and doing these jobs well, has been submerged by the preoccupation with "management", as if it was something quite distinct from these humdrum activities' FINANCIAL TIMES

'What ails the British economy, he claims, is not the quality of its management, but the fact that management exists at all' NEW STATESMAN

Gail Duff
Country Wisdom £1

An encyclopedia of recipes, remedies and traditional good
sense. The popular author of *Vegetarian Cookbook* and *Fresh
all the Year* has collected pages of fascinating folklore, herbal
recipes, traditional advice culled from centuries of country life.
Cures for everything from insomnia to toothache, hints for home
and kitchen, traditional good sense and entertainment on every
page.

Gavin and Bernard Lyall
Operation Warboard £1

How to fight World War II battles in miniature !

'Famous thriller writer Gavin Lyall and his son Bernard
combine forces to produce a very different wargames book which
focusses on battles of World War II in 20/25mm scale . . .
extremely readable' MILITARY MODELLING

Terence Reece and Albert Dormer
Bridge: The Acol System of Bidding 80p

ACOL is the bidding system used by eight out of every ten
bridge players — acknowledged by all bridge experts as the
fastest growing and most influential trend in the modern game.
Written by two top level tournament players, packed with
examples and practical advice, here is *the* guide to giving a
winning streak to your game.

Reference, Language and Information

All these books are available at your local bookshop or newsagent, or can be ordered direct from the publisher. Indicate the number of copies required and fill in the form below

Name⎯⎯⎯⎯⎯⎯⎯⎯⎯⎯⎯⎯⎯⎯⎯⎯⎯⎯⎯⎯⎯
(block letters please)

Address⎯⎯⎯⎯⎯⎯⎯⎯⎯⎯⎯⎯⎯⎯⎯⎯⎯⎯⎯

Send to Pan Books (CS Department), Cavaye Place, London SW10 9PG
Please enclose remittance to the value of the cover price plus:

25p for the first book plus 10p per copy for each additional book ordered to a maximum charge of £1.05 to cover postage and packing Applicable only in the UK

While every effort is made to keep prices low, it is sometimes necessary to increase prices at short notice. Pan Books reserve the right to show on covers and charge new retail prices which may differ from those advertised in the text or elsewhere